BLACKPOOL FC IN THE FOOTBALL LEAGUE

Who's Who 1896 to 1915

12.7.22
To Helen & Mark,
With Love,
Garth.

Garth Dykes and Mike Davage

A *SoccerData* Publication

Published in Great Britain by Tony Brown,
4 Adrian Close, Toton, Nottingham NG9 6FL.
Telephone 0115 973 6086. E-mail soccer@innotts.co.uk
www.soccerdata.com

First published 2022

Cover design by Bob Budd.

GARTH'S DEDICATION

With love to my great niece, Victoria Rose, and her partner of today's Blackpool FC, Matty Virtue

Printed and bound by 4Edge, Hockley, Essex
www.4edge.co.uk

ISBN: 978-1-911376-22-4

BLACKPOOL FC 1896 TO 1915

The senior clubs in Blackpool in the 1880s were South Shore and the first club to be called simply "Blackpool". This latter club were active from 1877 to 1887, entering the F.A. Cup in 1882-83 and 1883-84, and the Lancashire Senior Cup from 1880-81 to 1884-85. South Shore were the more successful of the two, beating Notts County on their way to the 6th Round of the F.A. Cup of 1885-86 in one of the early "giant killings" of Cup history. They applied unsuccessfully for League membership in 1889, and later joined the Lancashire League.

Today's Blackpool Football Club was created in late July 1887 when a handful of enthusiasts gathered together in a room in the Stanley Arms Hotel in Church Street. A formal resolution was passed that Blackpool Football Club should be formed, and, by doing so, gave birth to a club which, 43 years later, was to obtain First Division status. From its first inception rapid progress was the order of the day. The Lancashire Junior Cup and the Fylde Cup were won in the first successful season. They became founder members of the Lancashire League in 1890, and were champions four years later. In May 1896 the club was formed into a limited liability company with a capital of £2,000 in £1 shares and were elected to the Second Division of the Football League. However, the first balance sheet showed a loss of £1,182, despite everything having been done as economically as possible. Although the club's career was subsequently chequered owing to financial pressure, it succeeded in keeping its place in the Football League with the exception of a lapse for one season (1899-1900), during which time the Blackpool and South Shore organisations were amalgamated. The club's eventual financial improvement was in large part due to FA Cup-ties successes. In season 1905-06 Crystal Palace were defeated in round one after two replays in London and Birmingham. In the second round the club's directors accepted a sum of £250 plus a share of the gate, to transfer the game against Sheffield United to Bramall Lane, and, to general astonishment, they beat their First Division rivals by two goals to one. A share in a gate of over 35,000 at Newcastle United in round three was some real compensation following the heavy 5-0 defeat from the eventual finalists.

The seasons up to the outbreak of the First World War found Blackpool remaining in Division Two, with a highest finish of seventh in 1910-11. Re-election was necessary in 1909 and 1913. Their FA Cup record after 1906 was poor, reaching the third round on only one occasion up to 1914-15. In the Lancashire Senior Cup, the semi-finals were reached in 1899-1900, 1905-06 and 1912-13, and the final in 1913-14. On a dull and murky afternoon at Burnden Park in December 1913, Blackpool lost the final 0-1 to Manchester United. In the final season before League football was suspended for the duration of World War One, Blackpool ended with a flourish with eight wins and two draws from their final eleven matches.

The focus of this book is on the 241 players who represented Blackpool F.C. in Football League and FA Cup matches in the period commencing September 1896 and concluding in August 1915. A challenging period for the football historian but one that your authors' feel will have shed some new light on the already well documented history of the Blackpool Football Club.

NOTES ON THE TEXT

For each player we have attempted to provide the following information: full names, recognised playing position, height and weight, date and place of birth, and date and place of death. It should be mentioned here that the dates of birth and death of some players have been culled from registers that only record such events in three-month periods. Hence the use (for instance) of 'January quarter 1903' denotes a span of January/February/March of that year. Also included are each player's debut, full career and biographical details, and a breakdown of appearances made and goals scored. Every player who played in a Football League match or an F.A. Cup-tie has been included. Abbreviations have been kept to a minimum and are those in general use in works of this type:

App/s	Appearance/s
cs	close season
gl/s	Goal/s
q.v.	denoting a cross reference
FA	Football Association
FL	Football League
WW1	The First World War (1914-18)

ALLAN, Walter Lennie "Watty"
Inside forward
Born: Paisley, Renfrew, 24th December 1868
Died: Victoria Hospital, Blackpool,
1st November 1943
Debut v Middlesbrough (a) 28.12.01, lost 1-2
CAREER: Abercorn. Stockton 1888. Middlesbrough cs 1890. Stockton. Heywood Central 1892. Rotherham 1893. Fairfield (Manchester) cs 1893. Chorley May 1895. Stalybridge Rovers October 1895. Northfleet United 1896. Kettering February 1897. Berry's Association July 1897. Manchester City June 1898. Thames Ironworks January 1899. Loughborough November 1899. Watford August 1900. **Blackpool November 1901.**

As can be seen from the above career details, Watty Allan was not one to outstay his welcome anywhere. Commencing in Scotland, he then sampled Lancashire League football, Southern League fare and three relatively short spells in the Football League. His best return came with Loughborough (18 apps and six goals). He made little impression with Blackpool, four of his six outings ending in defeat, the penultimate one a heavy 7-2 defeat at West Bromwich Albion, the eventual champions of the Second Division. He lived at 2, St Annes Drive, Blackpool, and at the time of his death his occupation was given as a retired dentist.
Appearances: FL: 6 apps 0 gls Total: 6 apps 0 gls

ANDERSON, George 'Geordie' E.

Inside forward
5' 8" 12st 0lbs
Born: Leith, 26th March 1874
Died: Leith, 15th March 1948
Debut v Stockport County (h) 23.2.00, won 3-0
CAREER: Leith Athletic. St Bernard's February 1889. Blackburn Rovers October 1892. New Brighton Tower August 1897. Blackburn Rovers May 1898. New Brighton Tower March 1899. **Blackpool August to October 1899**. Blackburn Rovers September 1899. **Blackpool February 1901**. Cliftonville (Ireland) coach August 1905.

Geordie Anderson was first associated with Blackpool when they were operating in the Lancashire League, following their failed re-election application at the close of the 1898-99 season. After a third spell with Blackburn Rovers he returned to Blackpool, and while a veteran (in footballing terms) he was a most valuable member of the squad. A lengthy and uninterrupted run of appearances at inside right in 1901-02 paid dividends with thirteen goals in League and Cup, when the next highest scorers managed just six. Despite being fielded at centre half for much of the following season, his return of eight goals in 30 matches made him joint leading scorer in League matches. In a more familiar role of inside forward in his final season, his seven goals included the season's only hat trick scored by him against Burton United in a 4-1 victory on 20th February 1904.
Appearances: FL: 91 apps 29 gls FAC: 7 apps 1 gl Total: 98 apps 30 gls
Honours (Blackburn Rovers) Lancashire Cup winner 1896.

ANDERSON, Thomas
Inside left 5' 8" 12st 0lbs
Debut v Bristol City (h) 2.4.04, lost 0-1
CAREER: Clyde FC May 1903. **Blackpool March 1904**.

In a brief association with the Seasiders, Thomas Anderson's two consecutive appearances, within the space of two days, both resulted in defeat. The home defeat by Bristol City followed by a 4-0 defeat at Grimsby Town. Only a better goal average saved Blackpool from a re-election application, and Stockport County, with equal points, failed in their application for re-instatement, spending a successful season in the Lancashire Combination, and subsequent election back into Division Two for season 1904-05.
Appearances: FL: 2 apps 0 gls Total: 2 apps 0 gls

ANDERTON, William 'Billy'

Outside right
5' 7" 10st 10lbs
Born: Blackpool, 29th September 1879
Died: Fylde, July quarter 1942
Debut v Gainsborough Trinity (h) 21.12.01, won 3-0
CAREER: Blackpool Etrurians. Poulton. **Blackpool November 1901**. Accrington Stanley May 1904. Nelson June 1905. Darwen August 1906. Barrow October 1907. Colne AFC April 1908. Oswaldtwistle Rovers October 1908. Rossendale United November 1908. Blackpool Athletic March 1909.

Billy Anderton was born at Blackpool, and first played for Blackpool Etrurians. He then joined Poulton for a season and a half during which time they were champions of the Fylde League and winners of the local Medal Competition. He then joined Blackpool for three seasons. A fleet-footed wingman who centred with nice judgement, his first team appearances increased year on year, but he was allowed to depart after missing just one match in 1903-04. Joining Accrington Stanley, and then Nelson in the same season, he then returned to Blackpool, who had retained his registration. He featured mainly in the Reserve team in 1905-06, assisting them to promotion from Division Two of the Lancashire Combination as runners-up to Colne AFC. Retained for a further season, he was recalled for first team duty in November in the unfamiliar position of outside left, and netted the winning goal against West Bromwich Albion on his return. At the end of the season he was tranfer listed with a fee of £100 on his head, which led to an appeal to the Football League who reduced the fee to £5. He did not, however, find another League club, continuing in Lancashire Combination football, subsequently traced with Colne AFC playing at full back and partnering Wallace Lowe (q.v.)
Appearances: FL: 104 apps 10 gls FAC: 4 apps 2 gls Total: 108 apps 12 gls

APPLETON, Leonard 'Len'

Forward
5' 6½" 11st 6lbs
Born: Bamfurlong, 16th November 1892
Died: Whelley, Wigan, 20th August 1970
Debut v Birmingham (a) 28.11.14, lost 0-3
CAREER: Scowcroft's Colliery. Atherton. **Blackpool May 1914**. (Wartime guest player with Bolton Wanderers). Exeter City May 1920. Southport July 1921, retired May 1922.

Len Appleton was allowed time to develop in the Reserves after a trio of early appearances on the right wing as deputy for John Charles. His breakthrough came in early February when he was selected at inside right in place of Ben Green, the former Preston North End forward. In wartime football, apart from a spell with Bolton Wanderers, he assisted Blackpool in 55 matches. On the resumption of League football in 1919-20 he appeared in 15 matches, winding up his career with a season each with Exeter City and Southport. A former surface worker at a colliery, he was a keen bowler, finishing runner-up in the locally famous Talbot Bowling Tournament in Blackpool.
Appearances: FL: 18 apps 3 gls Total: 18 apps 3 gls

ATHERTON, Walter

Left half back 5' 10" 11st 6lbs
Born: Blackpool, 1st October 1874
Died: Blackpool, 4th November 1930, age 56
Debut v New Brighton Tower (h) 4.3.99, lost 1-2
CAREER: Blackpool Central. South Shore. **Blackpool 1890, registered for FL matches February 1899, retired July 1900.**

A January 1900 biography of Walter Atherton revealed that he had been with the Blackpool club for nine seasons. Originally operating as an inside left he commenced with Blackpool Central. On leaving this junior combination he played for South Shore in just three matches before joining Blackpool in 1890. It was during early days with Blackpool FC that

he played alongside Sir Lindsay Parkinson, who subsequently became Mayor of the town for three years between 1916 and 1919. He was also a honourary freeman, former MP for the Borough, and chairman and president of Blackpool FC. He was also the head of a firm of Government contractors that bore his name. By the time that Blackpool became a Football League club, Walter Atherton's business interests in town restricted his availability. Described as tricky, speedy and very constructive, he appeared in just eight Football League matches, when it was said that he had offered his services to the club as an amateur. His occupation in early days was listed as a 'stone worker', and later a 'refreshment house keeper'. Walter Atherton was a member of an old Blackpool family, his father was born in Blackpool and was a military tailor, his grandfather was also a tailor in Blackpool in the neighbourhood of West Street. At one time a director of Blackpool FC, he was a staunch and active Conservative, and took a great interest in the Wainwright Club, of which he was chairman for three years, from 1923 to 1926. A brother, Jimmy Atherton, was a professional footballer who played for South Shore, Leicester Fosse and Gillingham. Sadly, at the inquest into his death it was stated that Walter Atherton had committed suicide. Evidence showed that his daughter had found him gassed, after receipt of a letter from the bank that indicated financial concerns.
Appearances: FL: 8 apps 0 gls Total: 8 apps 0 gls

BADDELEY, Amos

Forward
5' 7" 10st 3lbs
Born: Fegg Hayes, 1st April 1885
Died: Sydney, NSW, Australia, 3rd November 1957
Debut v Barnsley (h) 2.9.08, drawn 1-1
CAREER: Fegg Hayes. Stoke November 1906. **Blackpool July 1908.** Stoke May 1909. Walsall May 1912. Abertillery. Ebbw Vale.

Amos Baddeley hailed from a family of twelve children – 10 boys and two girls. Three of the boys subsequently became professional footballers. Amos followed his brother George to the Victoria Ground in November 1906, and moved to Blackpool in July 1908. He was one of the Seasiders' better players in the season when they finished at the foot of Division Two, appearing in all but six matches during the campaign. He returned to Stoke and took his overall record in all competitions with the Potters to a very creditable 52 goals in 97 matches. Later he was the prorietor of a window cleaning business, and he subsequently emigrated to Sydney, Australia, in 1928, and died there at the age of 72 in November 1957. His brother George, a wing half back, appeared in 208 League matches for Stoke, and 145 for West Bromwich Albion. Brother Tom was a goalkeeper who played for Burslem Port Vale (62 matches), Wolverhampton Wanderers (296 matches) and Bradford Park Avenue (nine matches). He was capped by England five times and represented the Football League in four inter-league matches.
Appearances: FL: 32 apps 3 gls FAC: 2 apps 0 gls Total: 34 apps 3 gls

BAINBRIDGE, Joseph 'Joe'

Centre forward and right half back
5' 8½" 11st 0lbs
Born: Jarrow, 11th March 1888
Died: Blackpool, 20th October 1954
Debut v Gainsborough Trinity (h) 2.1.11, drawn 1-1
CAREER: South Shields Parkside. Newcastle United (trial). Blyth Spartans. **Blackpool November 1910.** Southport July 1921 to 1925. Eccles United 1926.

Joe Bainbridge's Blackpool career really took off in season 1912-13. Having started the season at wing half back, he reverted to his more usual position at centre-forward and scored six goals in his first seven outings as attack leader, prompting the 'Lancashire

Daily Post' to consider him the best centre forward the club had had for a long time. Despite his success, Bainbridge was back in the middle line in the following season, and in 1914-15 he enjoyed his first ever-present season. In August 1917 news reached Blackpool that Gunner Joseph Bainbridge had been badly wounded in his left arm and cheek by an exploding shell. Happily he recovered sufficiently to assist Blackpool Reserves to win the Central League championship in 1919-20, having been awarded a benefit of £300 in the previous season. Leaving in July 1921 to join Southport on their election to the Football League he appeared in 65 matches in four seasons, operating throughout as a full back. He later worked as a commissionaire at Blackpool Tower, an attendant at the Winter Gardens, and was a licensed victualler at the Brunswick Hotel.
Appearances: FL: 111 apps 11 gls FAC: 4 apps 0 gls Total: 115 apps 11 gls

BANKS, James
Inside/Outside right
Born: Blackpool
Debut v Luton Town (h) 30.4.98, won 1-0
CAREER: Blackpool March 1898. Parr FC March 1900. Blackpool St Paul's March 1901. Parr FC September 1902. Royston United February 1903. Grimethorpe October 1904.

In Blackpool's second season in Division Two, the directors arranged a friendly match against a 'Tradesman's Eleven' on 16th March 1898, in order to give trials to a number of promising local players. James Banks had shown sufficient skill in the match to warrant a run out with the League side in the final fixture of the season, a 1-0 win against Luton Town. Played in wretched weather, and with a 'gate' of less than 300 according to one observer. So heavy was the rainfall that the match was played for just 35 minutes each half and without an interval, and, at that, the players and spectators had seen more than enough. Retained for the following season, Banks had a fair amount of first team action in a very poor team that, despite a late rally that included home and away wins against Darwen and a 4-0 victory against Gainsborough Trinity, lost their Football League status when their re-election application proved unsuccessful.
Appearances: FL: 10 apps 0 gls FAC: 2 apps 0 gls Total: 12 apps 0 gls

BARCROFT, Thomas "Tom" Arthur

Goalkeeper
Born: Waterfoot, 9th August 1871
Died: Blackpool, 26th September 1946
Debut v Leicester Fosse (a) 15.3.02, lost 0-1
CAREER: Blackpool May 1901

Many years after making his emergency appearance in goal for Blackpool at Filbert Street, Leicester, Tom Barcroft was awarded the FA's long-service medal, in recognition of 21 years service as honorary secretary of the club, whose directors additionally presented him with a gold cigarette case. His outstanding emergency playing performance in goal at Leicester was one of the greatest surprises of the day, but his smartness owed something to his early experience of goalkeeping with the Blackpool Hockey Club. He was beaten only once at Leicester, and the goal caused great controversy at the time. Leicester Fosse were awarded a free kick near to Blackpool's goal, and while one of their players placed his foot on the ball, another (Swift) kicked it into the net. The referee awarded the goal, but obviously made a mistake, because the ball could not be legally played a second time until the first player had completely rolled the ball over. The rules stating that the penalty for kicking the ball before it had travelled 27 inches – the length of its circumference – is a free kick to the other side. In earlier days, Tom Barcroft moved from Rossendale to Blackpool in 1880 and for a time worked in the Blackpool Borough Treasurer's department, and later in a Blackpool bank. He became one of the best-known personalities in Lancashire football administration for half a century. He was a member of the Football League Management Committee for many years, and at one time president of the Lancashire Football Association. One

distinction that he had was that of being the only honorary secretary of a Football League club. For thirty years he held that post at Blackpool, seeing the club grow from a small start until it reached the First Division of the Football League. Tom Barcroft died at his home in Park Road, Blackpool, in September 1946 at the age of 75.
Appearances: FL: 1 app 0 gls Total: 1 app 0 gls

BATE, Thomas "Tom"

Outside left
5' 8" 12st 0lbs
Born: Golborne 1st October 1883
Died: Bamfurlong, near Wigan, 18th October 1920
Debut v Gainsborough Trinity (h) 16.9.05, drawn 2-2
CAREER: Brynn Central. **Blackpool May 1905**. Brynn Central September 1907. Garston Gasworks February 1908. Wallasey Village September 1908. African Royal November 1908. Wallasey Village August 1909.

Tom Bate, described as 'young, quick and sure on the ball' made a promising start with Blackpool, quickly winning the outside left berth after Eddie Darlington, the former Chorley wingman, had started the season as first choice. In mid term, however, he was critisied for carrying his trickery on the ball to excess, leading to his being robbed through trying to do too much on his own. He shone, however, on return to the Reserves, helping them to win promotion to the First Division of the Lancashire Combination as runners-up to Manchester City Reserves. Retained for a second season, he assisted the second team to establish themselves in the higher sphere by finishing in eleventh place in the table, but he was called upon for first team action on only three occasions. At the end of the campaign he returned to his first love, Brynn Central, of the Lancashire Combination Division Two. A colliery office clerk from school, he was working in a similar capacity for the Co-operative Society at the time of his tragically early death at the age of 37.

Appearances: FL: 18 apps 1 gl FAC: 3 apps 0 gls Total: 21 apps 1 gl

BAXENDALE, James Henry
Inside right
Born: Chorley, July quarter 1878
Debut v New Brighton Tower (a) 1.9.1900, drawn 0-0
CAREER: Southport Central May 1899. **Blackpool July 1900**. Barrow. St Helens Town May 1904. Atherton Church House May 1906. Barrow October 1907. Bacup September 1908.

It was hardly a surprise when Blackpool sought the services of James Baxendale from Southport Central, as in the previous season he had scored twice to knock Blackpool out of the FA Cup on 28th October 1899, and followed up with another brace when the teams met in a league match in the following month. Sadly, he failed to replicate his scoring touch on joining Blackpool despite appearing in eight of the first nine matches of the season. Baxendale was not alone in his failure in front of goal, however, as the team managed to score only 33 goals in the 34-match League programme. James Baxendale worked in a cotton mill from the age of 13, and, according to the 1911 Census, he was an electrician.
Appearances: FL: 10 apps 0 gls FAC: 2 apps 0 gls Total: 12 apps 0 gls

BEARE, George

Winger
5' 7" 10st 10lbs
Born: Shirley, Southampton, 2nd October 1885
Died: Cardiff, 31st January 1970
Debut v Barnsley (h) 2.9.08, drawn 1-1
CAREER: St Mary's Guild FC. Shirley Warren. Southampton amateur July 1906, professional April 1907. **Blackpool May 1908**. Everton November 1910. Cardiff City June 1914. Bristol City November 1921. Cardiff City June 1922. Oswestry Town November 1922 to May 1924, player-manager from December 1923.

George Beare had appeared in just one Southern League match for his hometown club, Southampton, but was quickly a fixture in Blackpool's front line. He was quite the star man in the Seasiders' attack in his first season, but his good work was not always backed up. He had appeared in all five forward positions at the time of his transfer to Everton, for whom he gave excellent service, scoring 19 goals in 118 League and Cup matches. Spells with Cardiff City and Bristol City took his overall career record to 217 League appearances and 41 goals. His hobbies included billiards and trick cycling! In 1939 he was employed as a night watchman.
Appearances: FL: 76 apps 18 gls FAC: 4 apps 0 gls Total: 80 apps 18 gls

BENNETT, Charles Richard

Forward 5' 8" 11st 4lbs
Born: Fleetwood, 1st July 1879
Died: Preston, 13th January 1939
Debut v Woolwich Arsenal (a) 5.9.03, lost 0-3
CAREER: Fleetwood Amateurs. Lytham FC. Fleetwood Rangers January 1899. **Blackpool May 1903**. Brynn Central August 1904. Lytham Institute October 1904. Accrington Stanley November 1904. **Blackpool July 1905**. Bradford City November 1905, fee £140. Oldham Athletic September 1906. Barrow November 1907. Kirkham February 1912.

In November 1905, a Blackpool correspondent wrote : "Considerable dissatisfaction was created at Blackpool yesterday by the news that the local directorate had transferred Bennett to Bradford City. Bennett is Blackpool's best forward, and the only man who has played in every match this season. He impressed the Bradford directors immensely when the 'Seasiders' appeared at Valley Parade on October 28th. The Yorkshire club gains a versatile recruit who dribbles speedily, passes accurately, and shoots with judgment and deadliness." Though, in fact, not very speedy, Bennett had excellent control of the ball and was a good shot. He began with Fleetwood Amateurs, after which he joined Lytham. When he was with the Amateurs they won the Amateur Cup, the Fylde League, and the Blackpool Medal Competition. It was while he was showing such good form in the latter competition that Blackpool signed him. Despite his excellent first season at Bloomfield Road, he decided not to re-sign and moved on, assisting Brynn Central and Accrington Stanley in 1904-05. He was welcomed back in July 1905 and scored four goals in his first six matches, form that attracted a bid of £140 from Bradford City and his much regretted departure from Bloomfield Road for the second time. After scoring three goals in 16 League and Cup matches he left Valley Parade at the end of his first season. He joined Oldham Athletic in September 1906 but made only one first team appearance, on the day following his transfer from Bradford City, in a Lancashire Cup replay against Darwen on 25th September. Thereafter he remained in the Reserves as the first team went on to win the championship of the Lancashire Combination Division One, and subsequent elevation to the Football League in 1907-08.
Appearances: 43 apps 13 gls FAC: 2 apps 0 gls Total: 45 apps 13 gls

BILLINGTON, Joseph 'Joe'
Outside right
Born: Kirkham, 7th July 1878
Died: Fylde, April quarter 1948 age 61
Debut v Leicester Fosse (a) 15.3.02, lost 0-1
CAREER: Kirkham F.C. **Blackpool amateur May 1901.**

Joe Billington's sole appearance at Leicester was made on a heavy pitch, and what was described as "a perfect hurricane of wind, blowing straight across the ground, giving little advantage to either side." His big opportunity came when a Fosse defender missed his kick close to goal, giving Billington an opening that he squandered, his shot passing well wide of goal. His debut was described as "disappointing" and while he had shone in the ranks of Kirkham, he was considered not yet good enough for League football. Blackpool had arrived with only ten men for the game, goalkeeper Dorrington having missed his train at Preston. Tom Barcroft, a member of the Blackpool Committee, stepped into the breach and for a

novice gave a very assured performance between the posts.
Appearances: FL: 1 app 0 gls Total: 1 app 0 gls

BIRCH, William 'Bill'

Outside left
5' 8" 10st 10lbs
Born: Rainford, near St Helens, 1st November 1887
Died: Eccleston, 14th June 1968
Debut v Leicester Fosse (a) 15.2.08, lost 1-2
CAREER: Atherton May 1907. **Blackpool February 1908**. Nottingham Forest May 1908. Reading May 1909. St Helens Town July 1910. Eccles Borough November 1911. Grimsby Town May 1912. Gainsborough Trinity May 1914. (Wartime guest player with Rotherham County) Steam Trawler Co. Charlton's (Grimsby).

By occupation a blacksmith, and "As hard as nails" according to one correspondent, Bill Birch's consistent displays with Atherton earned him a move to Blackpool in the late stages of season 1907-08. Immediately impressive, he netted the only goal of the game in his second appearance against Stoke, and further goals against Bradford City and Grimsby Town helped lift the team away from the lower reaches of Division Two. Sadly, Blackpool were unable to hang on to their star recruit, a £350 transfer fee taking him to Nottingham Forest of the First Division. As with Blackpool, Birch started brightly, scoring against Chelsea in his second appearance, but a ten-match winless run followed and he lost his first team place. A move to Reading proved unrewarding, as they were relegated from Division One of the Southern League, winning only seven of 42 League matches. He next figured in Division Two of the Lancashire Combination with Eccles Borough, but was then given another opportunity in League football by Grimsby Town, but they suspended him sine die for alleged misconduct after he had made 34 appearances and scored one goal.
Appearances: 13 apps 3 gls Total: 13 apps 3 gls

BIRCHALL, John 'Jack'

Left half back
5' 10" 12st 0lbs
Born: Prescot, 28th April 1876
Died: Prescot, 13th February 1945
Debut v New Brighton Tower (a) 1.9.00, drawn 0-0
CAREER: Prescot Ramblers. Whiston Ramblers. St Helens Recreation August 1897. Liverpool September 1898. **Blackpool August 1900**. Blackburn Rovers February 1903. Leyton (trial) September 1907.

During his three years with Blackpool Jack Birchall was widely recognised as the best half back the club had had for many a day. Birchall was born at Prescot and while playing with the St Helens club he came under the keen eye of Mr Tom Watson, the Liverpool manager. Although Mr Watson was to be complimented on signing Birchall, he made the mistake of not giving him a run out with the League side. When approached by Blackpool, he willingly allowed the player to go, and he settled immediately at Bloomfield Road. A commanding figure, fearless in the tackle and terrific in the air, he was the cornerstone of Blackpool's defence alongside usual half back partners, Harry Stirzaker and Edward Threlfall. Financial difficulties forced Blackpool to accept an offer from Blackburn Rovers for their talented defender who sadly failed to realise full expectations at Ewood, appearing in 40 League and Cup matches in a little over four years. Unfortunately, he suffered a broken leg at Sheffield Wednesday in November 1905, and made only one more League appearance before leaving in the summer of 1907. A trial with Leyton in October 1907 did not lead to a permanent engagement.
Appearances: FL: 81 apps 3 gls FAC: 4 apps 0 gls Total: 85 apps 3 gls

BIRKET, Robert Kirkham. 'Bob'

Utility
Born: Weeton, Lancs. 4th December 1878
Debut v Lincoln City (h) 14.11.96, won 3-1 (scored one goal)
CAREER: Fleetwood Rangers. **Blackpool July 1896, and re-signed August 1900**

On September 16th 1896, to honour an agreement with the Fleetwood Rangers club in regard to the transfer of Bob Birket, Blackpool took their full League team to the Copse to play a friendly against the Wyre Port boys. Some two months later, Birket scored on his debut in the Football League. For some time a centre forward, and scorer of 36 goals in one season, which constituted a record for the Lancashire League, he later played mainly at half back, and later still, with John Scott on his left, he guarded Blackpool's goal at full back. In 1904, by this time captain of the club, he took a well-earned benefit when Preston North End provided the opposition. At the conclusion of the match he was presented with a handsome tea and coffee service, Mr R.B. Middleton, secretary of Blackburn Rovers, and former secretary of Blackpool, made the presentation. Described as a resolute tackler and prompt feeder, he was one of the best players that Blackpool had in their earliest days, and was generally acknowledged to be one of the most gentlemanly. Sadly, injuries curtailed his final season with the club, 1906-07, but he was fit enough to turn out as referee when a Blackpool School's Eleven played Revoe School at Bloomfield Road in May 1907. Hailing from a family of 14 children, his birth was registered as just Robert, his mother's maiden name (Kirkham) was added later. In 1891 Bob was a Waterworks Office clerk. In 1901 a Water Rate collector and in 1911 he was Secretary and Agent of a Conservative Association and Club.
Appearances: FL: 219 apps 44 gls FAC: 20 apps 5 gls Total: 239 apps 49 gls

BOOTH, Robert 'Bobby'

Half back
5' 8" 11st 7lbs
Born: West Hartlepool, 22nd May 1892
Died: Lancaster, January quarter 1974
Debut v Grimsby Town (a) 3.9.12, drawn 1-1
CAREER: Spennymoor United. **Blackpool May 1912**. (Wartime guest player with Workington). Birmingham May 1920. Southend United July 1922. Swansea Town June 1923, fee £175. Merthyr Town March 1925. New Brighton May 1925 to May 1926. Fleetwood September 1926. Skelmersdale United. Peasley Cross Athletic August 1928.

Bobby Booth commenced as a 20 year-old wing half back with Blackpool, and at either side of World War One completed over a century of League and Cup appearances, including one ever-present season in 1912-13. "A very hard worker who never becomes ruffled" was one appraisal, but his feathers were ruffled when he was sent off, along with E. Bassett of Notts County, and suspended for a fortnight from 1st September 1914. Moving on to Birmingham in May 1920, he made only eight appearances, six of which came in the 1920-21 Second Division Championship side. A series of yearly moves followed and took in Southend United (28 apps, 1 goal), Swansea Town (36 apps 4 goals), Merthyr Town (13 apps, 1 goal) and New Brighton (12 apps and 1 goal).
Appearances: FL: 102 apps 4 gls FAC: 4 apps 0 gls Total: 106 apps 4 gl

BOULTON, Alfred 'Alf'

Right full back
5' 8½" 11st 8lbs
Born: Kirkham, July quarter 1879
Died: K.I.A. in France on 29th January 1916, age 37 years.
Debut v New Brighton Tower (a) 1.9.00, drawn 0-0
CAREER: Kirkham Grammar School. Kirkham F.C. Wesham F.C.1898. **Blackpool July 1899**. Accrington Stanley May 1902. Lytham Institute November 1904. Kirkham F.C. October 1905. Darwen November 1905. Kirkham F.C. October 1906. Kirkham & Wesham September 1912.

Alf Boulton's early career was spent in the company of Edward Threlfall (q.v.), both natives of Kirkham and teammates with both the Kirkham and Wesham clubs. Blackpool were operating in the Lancashire League when Boulton was signed, and during the whole of his three seasons with the club nothing save illness or injury kept him out of the first team. He was offered terms for a fourth season but declined, explaining that the only thing that he disliked about League football was the long distance travelling involved. Very often he would leave home in the early hours of Saturday morning, and only return in the small hours of the following day. Accrington Stanley, of the Lancashire Combination, proved more to his liking, and in his first season with the Reds he assisted them to the championship of the First Division, and to the runners-up spot in his second. In both seasons the club were awarded Sutcliffe Medals, awarded to the non-League club securing the highest position. When his football career ended he became secretary of the Kirkham Football Club, and he was also an active member of the Kirkham Golf and Cricket Clubs. Sadly, Alfred Boulton lost his life, killed in action while serving with the 9th Loyal North Lancashire Regiment in France. In November of the same year a dedication and unveiling of a memorial cross to the memory of the late Sgt, A. Boulton took place in the Wesham Parish churchyard. The inscription reading: "In loving memory of Alfred Boulton, Sergeant, of the 9th Battalion L.N.L. Regiment, who was killed in action on 29th January 1916, aged 37 years".
Appearances: 54 apps 1 gl FAC: 4 apps 0 gls
Total: 59 apps 1 gl

BOWMAN, Thomas 'Tommy'

Full back
5' 8" 11st 8lbs
Born: Annbank, Tarbolton, 26th October 1873
Died: Southampton, 27th August 1958
Debut v Lincoln City (a) 5.9.96, lost 1-3
CAREER: Annbank 1891. **Blackpool June 1896**. Aston Villa November 1897. Southampton May 1901. Portsmouth April 1904. Eastleigh Athletic August 1909. Retired cs 1912.

With gate receipts averaging only £27 per match, Blackpool were unable to afford to keep their outstanding defender Tom Bowman, who was transferred to Aston Villa for a then signifecant sum of £200 in October 1897, having never missed a match since his arrival from Annbank in June 1896. It was stated at the time that Bowman's terms with the Villa were £4 per week, all year round. Immediately at home in Division One, Bowman assisted Villa to consecutive League championships before moving south to join Southampton. With the Saints came further success in the form of consecutive Southern League championships and an appearance in the 1900 FA Cup Final. A move along the coast to Portsmouth was less successful, although they challenged strongly for the Southern League title in 1906-07, finishing as runners-up to Fulham. Three years of non-League soccer with Eastleigh Athletic, a team

from the Railway Carriage Works where he was employed, wound up his career, and he was later employed for many years on Southampton Docks.
Appearances: FL: 38 apps 2 gls FAC: 4 apps 0 gls Total: 42 apps 2 gls
Honours: (Aston Villa) FL Champions 1899 and 1900. (Southampton) FA Cup finalist 1902. Southern League champions 1903 and 1904.

BRADSHAW, Richard 'Dick'

Half back
5' 8" 11st 0lbs
Born: Padiham, October quarter 1889
Died: Chorley, 30th November 1925
Debut v Gainsborough Trinity (a) 17.4.09, lost 0-1
CAREER: Accrington Stanley April 1907. Padiham September 1908. **Blackpool March 1909.** Rossendale United September 1912. Blackburn Rovers March to June 1913. Rossendale United December 1913.

Richard Bradshaw hailed from a Padiham family of nine children, seven sons and two daughters, four of the sons becoming well known footballers: William (Blackburn Rovers), Ernest (Burnley), Richard (the subject of this biography) and Jack (Accrington Stanley). William, the England international was the most famous, and Jack, when he played for Accrington Stanley, was one of the best centre halves in the Lancashire Combination. Richard joined Blackpool from Padiham, and his displays in the last two matches of the season ensured that he would be retained for the following term. He did in fact remain for four years, his senior outings increasing year on year, with 1911-12 his best – 22 League and Cup matches. Ironically, in the opening month of the following season he was transferred to Rossendale United. Later in the same campaign he was transferred to Blackburn Rovers, but was released with a free transfer after just three months at Ewood. In 1911 he was employed as a tripe dresser.
Appearances: FL: 30 apps 0 gls FAC: 5 apps 0 gls Total: 35 apps 0 gls

BRADSHAW, Thomas 'Tom' Dickinson

Inside/Outside-right
5-' 8" 11st 12lbs
Born: Stalmine, Lancs. 15th March 1876
Died: Fleetwood, 4th October 1953
Debut v Newton Heath (a) 26.12.96, lost 0-2
CAREER: Lostock Hall. Preston North End August 1896. **Blackpool November 1896.** Sunderland May 1897, fee £60. Nottingham Forest January 1898, fee £120. Leicester Fosse March 1899. New Brighton Tower May 1900. Accrington Stanley March 1901. Swindon Town August 1901. Reading November 1901. Preston North End September 1902. Wellingborough May 1903. Southport Central June 1904. Earlestown December 1904. Lytham Institute January 1905. Workington February 1905. Leicester Fosse October 1905. Rossendale United March 1906. Lancaster September 1906. Glossop May 1907. Penrith November 1907. Peterborough City December 1907. Darlington August 1908. Darwen November 1908. West Stanley September 1911.

A glance at the career details above illustrates that short stays were Tom Bradshaw's lot. A lively but irresponsible character, he could be brilliant on his day and practically useless on others. Sunderland, however, saw enough of him to take him to Roker after Blackpool had given him his first opportunity in League football. The move earned him a £10 signing-on fee and wages of £3 in the playing season, and £2 in summer. The nearest he came to honours occurred with Nottingham Forest when he was reserve in their FA Cup final appearance of 1898. An all-round sportsman, he acted as professional to the Preston Cricket Club, and in 1906 obtained a coaching role at Harrow, working under the old Lancashire County player, George Baker. Bradshaw had serious character flaws, however, these included lapses in training, and a conviction

for wife beating in 1908 and, in the 1920s, he was charged for posing as a beggar.
Appearances: FL: 18 apps 5 gls FAC: 3 apps 0 gls Total: 21 apps 5 gls

BRINDLEY, Horace

Outside left
5' 9½"   11st 2lbs
Born: Knulton, Staffordshire, 1st January 1885
Died: North Stafford Royal Infirmary, Hartshill, 18th June 1971
Debut v Stockport County (a) 2.9.07, drawn 1-1
CAREER: Knulton Villa. Stoke November 1904. Norwich City January 1906. **Blackpool June 1907.** Crewe Alexandra September 1908. Queens Park Rangers August 1910. Luton Town March 1911. Lincoln City May 1911. Chester June 1914.

The first thirteen of Horace Brindley's eighteen Blackpool left wing appearances were made consecutively from the start of season 1907-08. He was replaced initially by John Waddington and finally by Bill Birch, a late season recruit from Atherton, who did so well in his thirteen appearances, that he earned Blackpool a very handy £350 when transferred to Nottingham Forest. Horace Brindley eventually reached Lincoln City, who had failed to gain re-election to Division Two after finishing at the foot of the table in 1910-11. He played in all 32 of the Imps Central League championship side in 1911-12, and remained for a further two seasons, scoring four goals in 50 League appearances. At the ouset of his career, he appeared in four League matches for Stoke, and made 24 Southern League appearances for Norwich City.
Appearances: FL: 17 apps 2 gls FAC: 1 app 0 gls Total: 18 apps 2 gls

BROOKES, James Samuel 'Sam'

Right half back
Born: Llandudno, October quarter 1877
Died: Leominster, Herefordshire, 18th April 1964
Debut: Bristol City (h) 7.9.01, lost 0-2
CAREER: Llandudno Swifts 1899-1900. Rhyl 1900-01. **Blackpool June 1901**. Rhyl October 1901.

With two Wales caps against England and Ireland in 1900, and a successful season with Rhyl, runners-up in the Combination, Sam Brookes nevertheless failed to realise expectations with Blackpool. On his debut against Bristol City, with no regular goalkeeper available and Stirzaker taking over between the posts, Brookes, according to the 'Lancashire Evening Post' was not at all successful at half-back. In what proved to be a brief stay, he was later tried at inside right, and finally at outside right when he scored his team's goal in the 1-3 defeat at Glossop on 3rd October. In the same month he was released and returned to Wales and Rhyl FC. Outside of the game he was employed as an engine driver.
Appearances: FL: 3 apps 1 gl Total: 3 apps 1 gl
International Honours: Wales International, 2 caps 1900.

BROWN, Albert

Centre forward
5' 11"   12st 6lbs
Born: Austrey, 1st April 1879
Died: Birmingham, 6th April 1955
Debut v Hull City (a) 24.3.06, drawn 2-2
CAREER: Fazeley Swifts. Atherstone Star. Brownhill Albion. Tamworth. Aston Villa February 1898. Southampton April 1901. Queens Park Rangers October 1902. Preston North End May 1904. **Blackpool March 1906.**

Nicknamed the 'Tamworth Sprinter" the highlight of Albert Brown's career came when he scored seven goals for Southampton against Northampton Town in an 11-0 win in December 1901. It included a hat trick in the first five minutes of the match. In the same season he scored four goals in eight FA Cup-ties as the Saints reached the final at Crystal Palace, losing after a replay to Sheffield United, the two matches attracting a total attendance of 109,982 spectators. After a spell with Queens Park Rangers, Brown joined Preston North End for their return to Division One after three years spent in the Second flight. Their opening fixture was at Villa Park, and Albert Brown celebrated with a goal against his previous employers in North End's 2-1 win. Sadly, his season was blighted by a cartilage injury that restricted him to 17 League appearances (six goals). In the following term, when North End finished runners-up, he was restricted to just five appearances (one goal) and was transferred to Blackpool in late season. His stay at Bloomfield Road was not extended after just three League outings in which he failed to reproduce his earlier form.
Appearances: FL: 3 apps 0 gls Total: 3 apps 0 gls
Honours: (Southampton) FA Cup finalists 1902.

BROWN, Norman Liddle
Forward 5' 7" 11st 0lbs
Born: Willington Quay, 30th January 1885
Died: Lewisham, January quarter 1938
Debut v Hull City (h) 6.9.13, drawn 2-2 (scored one goal)
CAREER: Willington Athletic April 1902. Sunderland November 1904. Brentford July 1907. Luton Town May 1908. Southend United June 1909. North Shields Athletic September 1910. Millwall Athletic November 1910. Newcastle City August 1911. North Shields Athletic August 1912. **Blackpool August 1913.**

Norman Brown was a useful winger and the great Billy Hogg's understudy at Roker Park for nearly three years, appearing in 29 League and Cup matches, scoring two goals. He then undertook a tour of Southern League clubs before returning to the North East in the shape of non-League football with Newcastle City and North Shields Athletic. Returning to League football with Blackpool, he scored in each of his first two appearances from centre forward but lost his place in the side when another ex-Sunderland player, Joe Lane, was signed and was immediately impressive, scoring 11 goals in 26 matches, and following with 28 goals in season 1914-15, at that time the best seasonal return of any Blackpool player.
Appearances: FL: 13 apps 2 gls Total: 13 apps 2 gls

BUCHAN, Thomas 'Tom' Murray

Inside forward
5' 9½" 11st 7lbs
Born: Plumsted, 16th September 1889
Died: St Andrews Hospital, Bow, 27th January 1952
Debut v Bury (h) 20.9.13, lost 0-1
CAREER: Woodhill Thistle.Leyton FC (trial). Sunderland Rovers December 1912. **Blackpool June 1913**. Bolton Wanderers May 1914. Tranmere Rovers June 1923. Runcorn cs 1924. Atherton October 1924. Runcorn (trial) June 1927. Bacup Borough 1928. Later a Lancashire Combination referee.

A brother of the celebrated Sunderland and England inside forward Charles Buchan, whose season with Blackpool was impressive enough to attract outside attention, Bolton Wanderers, of the First Division, signing him in May 1914. Sparily used in his first season at Burnden Park, Tom Buchan eventually totalled 117 League and Cup matches and 14 goals, highlights being an ever-present season in 1919-20 and a hat trick against Preston North End on Christmas Day 1919. As the Wanderers contested the first Wembley Cup Final and a 2-0 win against West Ham United, Tom Buchan departed Burnden Park, ending his League career with a season at Tranmere Rovers of the Third Division North. Operating at wing half back he made 36 League appearances, one of which, on 12th January, marked the debut of 16 year-old 'Dixie' Dean, whose 27 goals in as many

matches in the following season earned him an upward move to Everton, and subsequent international fame and a career total that included 43 hat tricks.
Appearances: FL: 24 apps 2 gls Total: 24 apps 2 gls

BURDEN, John Robert

Left full back
5' 11" 12st 4lbs
Born: Liverpool, 20th March 1874
Died: 1941 (Burial 11th February)
Debut v New Brighton Tower (a) 1.9.1900, drawn 0-0
CAREER: St Aidan's College (Birkenhead). Tuebrook A.F.C. Everton Amateurs. Everton F.C. Reserves. South Liverpool August 1898. **Blackpool August 1900.** Chorley September 1902. St Helens Recreation October 1904. Earlestown May 1906.

John Burden captained Tuebrook A.F.C. for two seasons, his partner at full-back, W. Balmer, subsequently starring with England and Everton (293 League appearances). A memento of his partnership came in the form of a treasured gold medal. A four-month spell with Everton Amateurs led to a spell with Everton, whose reserve team he assisted. A season with South Liverpool in the Lancashire League followed, and his good form led to his signing by Blackpool. After appearing in all but four matches in his first season, a breakdown in his health in early season led to a 14 week lay off and he was unable to regain his place in the side when recovered. Released in the close season he had decided to retire from playing but was persuaded to prolong his career by Chorley, where an early match report praised his "Sure and strong kick, and the general enthusiasm that characterised his play." John Burden was a master blacksmith by trade.
Appearances: FL: 35 apps 0 gls FAC: 1 app 0 gls Total: 36 apps 0 gls

BURKE, Patrick 'Pat' M.M.

Half back
5' 8" 11st 0lbs
Born: Hebburn-on-Tyne, 6th March 1890
Died: 1942
Debut v Lincoln City (a) 19.10.12, lost 0-1
CAREER: Hebburn Argyle. **Blackpool May 1912**. Darlington Forge Albion 1919. Darlington June 1921. Reyrolles FC December 1922.

In five Football League seasons, at either side of the Great War, Pat Burke spent practically the whole of his first three years in the Reserves, finding more opportunities when League football resumed in 1919-20, the season in which he was awarded a benefit of £300. He departed at the end of the following season, returning to the North East for a final season in League football with Darlington, assisting the Quakers to finish as runners-up to Stockport County for the championship. While there was every reason to congratulate the club at the conclusion of their first season in the newly constituted Northern Section of the Third Division, on the financial side they showed a loss of £2,437, in part a result of trade depression and reduced attendances. While serving as a Sergeant in the Royal Field Artillery during WW1, Pat Burke was twice wounded and was awarded the Military Medal in 1917. He subsequently followed his Irish father as a shipyard worker with builders Hawthorne Leslie.
Appearances: FL: 19 apps 0 gls Total: 19 apps 0 gls

BURT, John

Centre forward
6' 0"   12st 0lbs
Born: Guildford, 25th November 1888
Died: 1960
Debut v Lincoln City (a) 9.10.09, drawn 2-2 (scored one goal)
CAREER: Bishopstoke FC. **Blackpool April 1909.**

An article in the 'Hampshire Chronicle' of 29th May 1909 ran as follows:"During the last three seasons the Bishopstoke club have won nine cups and 94 medals, their record being: P 98 W 80 L 14 D 4 Goals for 415, against 78. During this period John Burt has scored 101 goals, including 44 in the last season. He has signed for Blackpool for next season." The ideally built 20 year-old proved enthusiastic and powerful and netted in each of his first two appearances in the League side, but spent the majority of the season in the Reserves, assisting them to promotion from Division Two of the Lancashire Combination, twice recording double hat tricks in a season when the goals kept on coming, 118 being recorded in the 38 match tournament. In the following season goals proved harder to come by (52 scored in 38 matches) and Burt made just one senior appearance, a 0-2 defeat at Gainsborough Trinity proving to be his last in senior football.
Appearances: FL: 7 apps 2 gls Total: 7 apps 2 gls

CAHILL, Richardson 'Richard' Gibbins
Outside right   5' 7"   11st 0lbs
Born: Sunderland, 17th February 1885
Died: Sunderland, April quarter 1949, age 64
Debut v Bradford Park Avenue (h) 16.9.11, lost 0-4
CAREER: Ryhope Villa May 1906.Houghton Rovers December 1907. **Blackpool May 1911**. Houghton Rovers September 1914.

Although said to have caused many problems for Lancashire Combination defences, it was not until December that Richard Cahill enjoyed an extended run in the League side that included four FA Cup-ties that ended with the February 3rd visit to Burnden Park where Bolton Wanderers won 1-0 before an attendance of 18,651 spectators. The fact that Cahill failed to register a goal during the season was indicative of the team's failure in front of goal, only 32 being scored in 38 League matches.
Appearances: FL: 20 apps 0 gls FAC: 4 apps 0 gls Total: 24 apps 0 gls

CARDWELL, George
Left full back
Born: Blackpool, 21st January 1876
Died: Blackpool, 28th November 1939
Debut v Leicester Fosse (a) 6.11.97, lost 1-4
CAREER: **Blackpool August 1897.**

The son of a bricklayer, George Cardwell was a plumber by trade and a reserve full-back for the Seasiders during season 1897-98. It was hoped that, following the sale of star full back Tommy Bowman to Aston Villa, that Cardwell would be capable of capably filling his position. However, a difficult debut at Leicester, and a subsequent leg injury resulted in solution being found when Harry Stirzaker was switched from centre half to left full back to partner the durable veteran, Harry Parr.
Appearances: FL: 5 apps 0 gls Total: 5 apps 0 gls

CARTHY, John
Centre forward   5' 8"   11st 7lbs
Born: West Derby, Liverpool, 25th January 1880
Died: Wallasey, 1st September 1945.
Debut v Leicester Fosse (h) 7.11.03, lost 1-2 (scored)
CAREER: Blackburn Rovers September 1902. **Blackpool November 1903.** Stalybridge Rovers July 1904. Egremont Social September 1905. Wallasey Village September 1908. Lingdale September 1909. Rochdale January 1910. Egremont September 1910. Aberdare June 1912. Seaton Delaval February 1913. Egremont March 1914.

Although John Carthy was a scorer on his Football League debut, he failed to add to his tally with Blackpool and spent the remainder of his career on non-League circles. A return to Lancashire with Rochdale saw him score on his debut in a friendly match against

Blackpool Reserves, followed by three goals in nine Lancashire Combination fixtures. By vocation he was a house painter and decorator.
Appearances: FL: 14 apps 1 gl Total: 14 apps 1 gl

CARTMELL, James 'Scotty'
Inside-right
Debut v Glossop (a) 3.9.98, lost 1-4
CAREER: Fleetwood Rangers November 1896, and re-signed July 1897. **Blackpool May 1898.**

Blackpool commenced season 1898-99 with four consecutive defeats, but one of many team changes saw Cartmell reintroduced in place of Harrison at outside right for the visit of Loughborough on 8th October. The 2-1 victory that ensued was Blackpool' first win of the season that ended in relegation from Division Two. The attendance at the Athletic Ground was estimated to be 500 spectators and the poor level of support throughout the season was doubtless a factor in the club's failure to gain re-election. After a lengthy spell out of the first team picture, Cartmell returned to play in six of the last seven matches of the campaign when a revival brought three wins and a draw, including a 6-0 home win against Darwen and a 4-0 victory against Gainsborough Trinity, insufficient in the event to take them clear of the re-election places.
Appearances: FL: 12 apps 1 gl Total: 12 apps 1 gl

CATTERALL, Alfred 'Alf' Vincent
Outside left
Born: Kirkham, January quarter 1881
Died: Poulton-le-Fylde, 29th July 1925, age 44
Debut v Burslem Port Vale (a) 15.12.1900, lost 0-4
CAREER: Kirkham. **Blackpool September 1900.**

When Alf Catterall was signed by Blackpool it was noted in the local press that his arrival made up a trio of players from Kirkham, Boulton and Threlfall being the other two. The extreme wing positions were the most troublesome that the Blackpool committee had ever had to contend with in a season when Blackpool registered only 33 goals in 34 League matches – the lowest total throughout the Football League. The youthful Catterall was expected to challenge for a place in the League side, but he was destined for a season in the Reserves after a difficult debut and a heavy defeat at Port Vale. The son of a seed merchant, Alf followed his father in the family business.
Appearances: FL: 1 app 0 gls Total: 1 app 0 gls

CHADWICK, Edgar Wallace "Hooky"

Inside left
5' 7" 11st 6lbs
Born: Blackburn, 14th June 1869
Died: Blackburn, 14th February 1942
Debut v Leicester Fosse (h) 3.9.04, drawn 0-0
CAREER: Little Dots FC 1884. Blackburn Olympic 1886. Blackburn Rovers cs 1887. Everton April 1897. Burnley June 1899. Southampton August 1900. Liverpool May 1902. **Blackpool May 1904**. Glossop May 1905. Darwen July 1906, retired 1908. Netherlands head coach October 1908 to November 1913, also coached The Hague & Harlem FC. England Amateur Team coach November 1908. Stonehurst College coach October 1912. Vitesse head coach 1914. Sparta Rotterdam head coach 1915. One final playing appearance at outside left for Blackburn Rovers in November 1916, at the age of 47.

After a season with Blackburn Rovers Edgar Chadwick joined Everton for the 1888-89 season and their debut in the newly formed Football League. He stayed at Goodison for eleven seasons, making exactly 300 League and Cup appearances, scoring 110 goals. Along the way, he won a League Championship medal and appeared in two FA Cup Finals. He won seven England Caps, scoring against Scotland in April 1892 after just 35 seconds. In the FA tour to Germany in November 1899, he scored ten goals in three matches. During his spell in the Southern League with Southampton, he won a Championship medal, but an FA Cup winners' medal continued to elude him as he was on the losing side in the 1902 Final, as he had been in his two Finals with Everton. Although well into the veteran stage on joining Blackpool he proved to be one the best signings made by the Blackpool committee as he appeared in every League and Cup match throughout the season, excelling in combination, additionally heading the scoring list. Edgar's cousin, Arthur Chadwick, played for and managed several League clubs and won two England caps while a Southampton player. On retirement, Edgar returned to Blackburn and his original trade as a baker.
Appearances: FL: 34 apps 8 gls FAC: 6 apps 3 gls Total: 40 apps 11 gls (Played in every match during the season, always at inside left)
Honours: England International, 7 caps, 1891 to 1897. FL Representative, 3 apps, 1891-1897. FA Tour to Germany November 1899. (Everton): FL Champions 1891. FA Cup Finalists 1893 & 1897. (Southampton): Southern League Champions 1901, FA Cup Finalists 1902.

CHAPMAN, Richard

Inside right
5' 7" 11st 0lbs
Born: Blackburn, 19th April 1892
Died: Blackburn, January quarter 1965
Debut v Grimsby Town (h) 9.9.12, won 2-1
CAREER: Blackburn Trinity. Blackburn Rovers. Blackburn Trinity. **Blackpool May 1912**. Stalybridge Celtic August 1914.

A youthful inside or outside right with some experience in the reserve team of Blackburn Rovers, Richard Chapman continued as a reserve team player on joining Blackpool. Moving on to Stalybridge Celtic – at that time members of the Southern League Second Division – he assisted them to the runners-up position, one point behind the champions, Stoke. He was working as a cotton spinner at Hornby's Brookhouse Mill at the time of his enlistment in the King's Liverpool Regiment, 27th Battalion. He was promoted to Lance Corporal in July 1918, but was absent without leave between 20th and 27th December in the same year and lost his stripe. He was discharged in March 1919.
Appearances: FL: 2 apps 0 gls Total: 2 apps 0 gls

CHARLES, John William

Outside right
5' 7½" 11st 2lbs
Born: Crook, 10th March 1890
Debut v Grimsby Town (a) 3.9.12, drawn 1-1
CAREER: Crook Town. **Blackpool May 1912 to 1924**.

22 goals for Crook Town in season 1911-12 paved the way for John Charles' entry into League football. Billed as 'the most likely looking candidate for the outside right berth' he certainly lived up to expectations when he

commenced with an ever-present season and a total of 108 League and Cup appearances and 18 goals before League football was suspended for the duration of the Great War. A clever dribbler with plenty of pace who centred the ball accurately, he had lost none of his attributes when normal League fare returned, his lengthy service rewarded with a benefit of £300 in season 1919-20. He was appointed assistant trainer when Major Frank Buckley took over as manager, remaining available as a player where necessary. In the event, six early season appearances wound up his long career. Fittingly his final outing against Crystal Palace at Bloomfield Road on 29th September resulted in a 2-0 victory, Blackpool's first of the season.
Appearances: FL: 234 apps 30 gls FAC: 13 apps 0 gls Total: 247 apps 30 gls

CHARLTON, Thomas 'Tommy'

Inside forward
5' 7" 11st 6lbs
Born: Hexham-on-Tyne, January quarter 1889
Died: Durham North West, January quarter 1949, age 60
Debut v Leeds City (h) 22.11.13, drawn 2-2
CAREER: Middlesbrough August 1907. Darlington July 1908. Stockport County May 1909. Burnley March 1913, fee £650. **Blackpool November 1913.**

Tommy Charlton was born at Hexham-on-Tyne but brought up in Middlesbrough He made his League debut with Stockport County, remaining for four seasons. He played in every position in the attack, but his skill and bustle was perhaps best utilised at inside forward. A noted scorer from the penalty spot, he could always be relied upon for a full 90 minutes performance. After scoring 29 goals in 99 appearances he was transferred to Burnley but failed to establish a regular place, despite scoring three goals in seven appearances. Said to have cost a record fee when signed by Blackpool, he immediately formed a productive forward partnership with centre forward Joe Lane, another new signing from Sunderland. Sadly, in the match against Leicester Fosse at Bloomfield Road on Good Friday, April 1914 Tommy Chapman suffered a fractured skull following an accidental collision with an opponent. Confined at the Victoria Hospital in Blackpool he made an almost miraculous recovery but when discharged in June he was still unable to walk unsupported. The club retained his services, although it seemed extremely doubtful that he would be sufficiently well to play again in the coming season. His football career was, in fact, over and he was said to have suffered some paralysis in his later years.
Appearances: FL: 22 apps 3 gls FAC: 1 app 0 gls Total: 23 apps 3 gls

CLARKE, John
Centre forward 5' 10½" 12st 7lbs
Born: Glasgow, 18th December 1872
Debut v Walsall (h) 13.2.97, won 3-2 (scored one goal)
CAREER: Busby Victoria 1889. Glasgow Rangers (trial) November 1890. Manchester Fairfield 1894. Bury April 1896, **Blackpool January 1897, fee £60** Luton Town May 1897, fee £60.

In November of his second season with Busby Victoria, John Clarke was offered a trial with Glasgow Rangers, this consisting of an appearance in a Glasgow Cup-tie against Queen's Park, which the Rangers won 4-2. In the following season he crossed the border to join Manchester Fairfield. Later with Bury, he appeared in an inter-county match, Lancashire v West Yorkshire, but played in little first team football (six matches). He was not short of admirers, however, in December 1896 executives of the Glossop club were in negotiations for his services, but no agreement was reached. In the following month he joined Blackpool, but after netting six goals in 13 matches, no agreement on terms for a new contract could be reached. He moved on to Luton Town for their first season in Division Two, but after an early debut against Woolwich Arsenal on 2nd October he did not feature again in the League side.
Appearances: FL: 13 apps 6 gls Total: 13 apps 6 gls

CLARKE, Tom

Left half back
5' 7½" 11st 2lbs
Born: Bury, April quarter 1881
Debut v Gainsborough Trinity (a) 29.9.06, lost 0-2
CAREER: Chorley August 1905. **Blackpool May 1906**. Nelson cs1912 to May 1913.

A model of consistency throughout his six seasons and as one observer reported: "A sturdily built player, clever and resourceful, who has taken to League football right away". At the end of his first season, and to mark his marriage to Miss Laura Foster in Lancaster, players and supporters of the club presented him with a large and handsome black-marble timepiece, bearing a suitable inscription. Having spent most of his final season in reserve he was released to join Nelson, whom he assisted to finish in third place in Division One of the Lancashire Combination in 1912-13. He was offered terms by the East Lancashire club for a second season but declined, and it was stated at the time that he intended to settle in Canada.
Appearances: FL: 137 apps 0 gls FAC 4 apps 0 gls Total: 141 apps 0 gls

CLARKE, William 'Bill'
Inside left
5' 6" 11st 3lbs
Born: Newcastle
Debut v Bradford P A (h) 16.9.11, lost 0-4
CAREER: Jarrow Caledonians. **Blackpool April 1911**. Hebburn Argyle November 1912.

One of several players with the club hailing from the North East, the 'Lancashire Daily Post Handbook 1912-13' considered him "Clever, but handicapped by lack of inches." Bill Clarke appeared in two wins and two defeats in early season, but did not reappear in the League side until January, when he scored in a 3-1 home win against Fulham on the 27th of the month. He then held his place in the side and appeared at Bolton Wanderers in the Second Round FA Cup-tie, won 1-0 by the First Division side.
Appearances: FL: 8 apps 1 gl FAC: 1 app 0 gls Total: 9 apps 1 gl

CLARKIN, John

Outside-right
Born: Neilston, Renfrew, 3rd April 1872
Debut v Lincoln City (a) 5.9.96, lost 1-3
CAREER: Neilston F.C. Bootle 1892. Glasgow Thistle July 1893. Newton Heath January 1894. **Blackpool June 1896 to May 1898.**

John Clarkin was one of Newton Heath's more successful early recruits from Scotland, but his five goals in 12 appeaqrances at the close of 1893-94 could not prevent the Heathens from experiencing relegation for the first time. In Division Two in the following season he missed only one match and scored eleven goals from the right wing. He was similarly consistent in 1895-96 scoring seven goals in 26 matches. He was signed by Blackpool in preperation for their first season in the Football League. In his second season a proposed transfer to Burnley came out very well for the Blackpool club. On the morning of May 4th, Burnley directors had agreed to pay £90 for his transfer, signed all the necessary papers, and paid Clarkin £5 as part-bonus money. On the same evening the Burnley club changed their mind and announced that the arrangements were off. Blackpool reported the matter to both the Football League and the Football Association, who ruled in Blackpool's favour in the matter – they kept the player and the £90, and Clarkin retained his £5! Clarkin signed off by scoring Blackpool's winning goal in the season's final fixture at the Athletic Grounds, Stanley Park, against Luton Town. In 1901 he was working as a bleacher.
Appearances: FL: 56 apps 11 gls FAC: 4 apps 0 gls Total: 60 apps 11 gls

CLENNELL, Joseph 'Joe'

Inside left
5' 5½" 11st 4lbs
Born: New Silksworth, 19th February 1889
Died: Blackpool, 28th February 1965
Debut v Leeds City (a) 3.9.10, won 2-1
CAREER: Silksworth United, Seaham Harbour. Seaham White Star November 1908. **Blackpool May 1910**. Blackburn Rovers April 1911. Everton April 1914. Cardiff City October 1921. Stoke February 1925. Bristol Rovers July 1926. Rochdale October 1927 to March 1928. Ebbw Vale player-manager March 1928. Barry Town player-manager September 1928. Bangor player-coach July 1929. Belfast Distillery manager October 1930. Great Harwood manager April 1913. Accrington Stanley coach 1934.

Clever at close dribbling and feared as a marksman, Joe Clennell scored 30 goals for Seaham Harbour in the season prior to his arrival at Bloomfield Road. After a relatively quiet start to life in Division Two he embarked on a prolific run of ten goals in as many matches. Although he departed to First Division Blackburn Rovers in April, his 18 League goals did much to propel Blackpool into seventh position in Division Two, the team's best ever placing at that point. Two first Division championships and three appearances for the Football League were highlights in Clennell's subsequent career in which he scored a total of 112 League goals in 309 appearances. Sadly, Joe Clennell lost his life in a road accident, being knocked down by a car while attempting to cross Norbreck Road in Blackpool.
Appearances: FL: 32 apps 18 gls FAC: 1 app 1 gl Total: 33 apps 19 gls
Honours: FL Representative, 3 appearances; twice versus the Scottish League 22nd February 1919 (Victory Match) and on 5th April 1919. Versus the Irish League on 19th November 1919. (Blackburn Rovers) FL Champions 1912. (Everton) FL Champions 1915.

COLLIER, James
Centre forward
Debut v Bradford City (a) 3.11.06, lost 0-3
CAREER: Atherton Church House. Fleetwood Amateurs. **Blackpool amateur November 1906.**

In November 1906, the 'Lancashire Evening Post' reported as follows: "For the trip to Bradford City, a trial is being given to a centre forward named Collier, of Fleetwood Amateurs, a young player who is highly spoken of, and who, last year, assisted Atherton Church House." The newcomer was afforded a bare three opportunities to improve Blackpool's shot shy attack, whose best marksman throughout the season was another amateur, W.A. Grundy, who notched the first of his eight goals in Collier's second appearance, a 2-1 victory against West Bromwich Albion on 10th November.
Appearances: FL: 3 apps 0 gls Total: 3 apps 0 gls

COLVILLE, George
Right half
Born: Annbank, Tarbolton, Ayr, 18th March 1876
Died: Glossop, 24th August 1928
Debut v Woolwich Arsenal (h) 4.1.97, drawn 1-1
CAREER: Annbank July 1895. **Blackpool June 1896**. Annbank 6th October 1897. Glossop North End 4th May 1898. Fulham December 1903 to cs 1904. Annbank. Port Glasgow Athletic cs 1908.

Collier George Colville began with Annbank, which, at the turn of the century, was described as a one-street village, but it certainly turned out many class footballers. Its Peeble Park pitch was sometimes named 'The Precipice' – usually by disgruntled opponents, but Annbank played as well away as they did at home. Colville first crossed the border to join Blackpool, but as deputy to Alec Stuart in the Seasiders first season in League football found few opportunities. His second spell in English football proved far more rewarding, particularly with Glossop, for whom he appeared in 112 League and Cup matches before a broken leg in 1901-02 halted his progress. A brother, James, was a Newton Heath player in season 1892-93.

Appearances: FL: 5 apps 0 gls FAC: 3 apps 0 gls Total: 8 apps 0 gls

CONNOR, James 'Jimmy'

Half back
5' 8½" 12st 7lbs
Born: Slamanan near Falkirk, Stirlingshire, 9th April 1881
Died: Blackpool, October quqrter 1940.
Debut v Burton United (h) 2.9.05, won 2-0 (Scored both goals)
CAREER: Parkhead F.C. Bathgate F.C. **Blackpool May 1905 to 1915.**

An article in the 'Scottish Referee' in June 1905 revealed that only one player whom the Bathgate club were desirous of retaining, Jimmy Connor, had migrated to Blackpool. One of Bathgate's best half backs, he left Mill Park as the club entered into the Scottish Combination, becoming the only East of Scotland club in the League. Earlier he had been member of the Parkhead team that won the Glasgow League and Cup. With Threlfall well established at right half in the Blackpool team, Connor was first tried at inside right, and in what proved to be an outstanding Blackpool career, he netted both goals on his debut in the first fixture of 1905-06. An early blot on his record was a fourteen day suspension by the FA after he had come to blows with a fellow Scot, Manchester United full back Bob Bonthron. A whole-hearted and energetic forward who had the happy knack of creating countless opportunities for his colleagues, he was first tried at left half back in 1907-08, later switching to centre half from 1910-11. It was not until his final season, 1914-15, that he lost his first team place to the emerging talents of George Wilson, who went on to win twelve England caps. Like his father, Jimmy Connor was a coalminer. He married Clara Evans in Fylde in July 1914, and in October of the following year enlisted in the Army Motor Transport Service.

Appearances: FL: 301 apps 29 gls FAC: 17 apps 0 gls Total: 318 apps 29 gls

COOK, Lawrence 'Lol' Whalley

Centre forward
5' 10" 12st 7 lbs
Born: Preston, 28th March 1884
Died: Wigan, 2nd December 1933
Debut v Glossop (h) 3.12.04, won 4-1
CAREER: Nelson. Lytham Institute. **Blackpool August 1904**. Nelson October 1905. Preston North End November 1905. Nelson December 1905. Lancaster May 1906. Southport Central September 1907. Gainsborough Trinity September 1908. Rossendale United December 1908. Bacup September 1910. Chester May 1911. Stockport County May 1912. Chester September 1913.

In a September 1904 article about Blackpool's troublesome centre forward position, the 'Lancashire Evening Post' commented: "Cook, of the Combination team, is without doubt a good goal scorer. The question is whether he would repeat his success in the League side. He is a bustler, and might probably rush goals through. If Hogg does not improve in the immediate future, maybe Cook will be promoted." In the event, he was given an opportunity but failed to score in nine appearances. Incidentally, it seemed strange that a forward line containing, as it did, an England International (Chadwick), an Irish international (Kearns), a Scottish junior international (McEwan), and a Football League championship winner (Hogg), should prove collectively to be so ineffective. The fact that Cook had scored four goals in his first match for Blackpool Reserves, who won 6-1 against Lytham suggested that he had something to offer, and in a wandering path he did score lots of goals on non-League circles. His overall League career, however, was less impressive – seven goals in 30 matches for four different clubs. As a cricketer, his record was far more impressive – 206 first class matches for Lancashire with 2,126 runs and 839 wickets. His best bowling performance was 8 for 39 versus

Northampton in 1911, and he also took seven Derbyshire wickets for just eight runs in 1920. He also played in Lancashire League cricket and once took nine wickets for nine runs for Penwortham and finished on the losing side! Lol's brother, Billy Cook had eleven first class matches for Lancashire and as a full back made 171 League and Cup appearances for Oldham Athletic between 1909-20 and was a Football League representative in 1919. Other brothers included James, who played in Minor Counties cricket with Cheshire and Durham, John also played for Cheshire
Appearances: 7 apps 0 gls FAC: 2 apps 0 gls Total: 9 apps 0 gls

COOKSON, Walter 'Wally' Stanley

Inside forward
5' 7" 11st 7lbs
Born: South Shore, 6th September 1879
Died: Surrey, January quarter 1948
Debut v Burslem Port Vale (a) 6.9.02, drawn 1-1
CAREER: Preston North End (trial) 1897. Skerton F.C. July 1899. Nelson May 1900. Bristol City July 1901. **Blackpool June 1902.** Wellingborough Town 1903, re-signed May 1904. Brentford May 1905. Portsmouth May 1906. **Blackpool September 1907.** Huddersfield Town August 1908. Burnell's Ironworks September 1909. Mersey Ironworks July 1911. Hoyland United August 1914.

Said to be relative of an old Blackpool player, at 18 years of age Wally Cookson was given a trial with Preston North End. In the following season he joined Skerton and on that club's disbandment, several clubs sought his services. He joined Nelson upon their re-entering the Lancashire League, and never missed a match in his first season. The following season saw him at Bristol City, where he was second highest goal scorer. Returning to his native town he had an excellent season, being very quick on the ball and with an eye for goal. At the end of the season he was one of six players who left Bloomfield Road, "Having succumbed to Southern attractions" according to one correspondent. Some four years later he returned to native parts but was unable to replicate his earlier success. He was living in Surrey when called up in April 1916, and served as an Engineer Sapper with the London Field Company. Subsequently promoted to Corporal he served in India and South Africa prior to his discharge in October 1918.
Appearances: FL: 34 apps 9 gls FAC: 2 apps 1 gl Total: 36 apps 10 gls

COPESTAKE, Levi
Winger 5' 5½" 10st 0lbs
Born: Kiveton Park, 28th September 1886
Died: Exeter, April quarter 1968
Debut v Barnsley (a) 21.4.06, drawn 1-1
CAREER: Kiveton Park amateur 1901, professional February 1905. Worksop North End October 1905. Worksop Town November 1905. **Blackpool April 1906.** Bristol City August 1907. Exeter City May 1908. Bristol City May 1910, & re-signed September 1911. In 1945 he was with Exeter City as Youth Coach.

In April 1904 the 'Sheffield Evening Telegraph' reported: "Worksop have transferred Levi Copestake to Blackpool. He played for Kiveton Park last season and then joined Worksop North End, and played in only one or two matches. Worksop signed him in November and he played at inside right until a week or two ago, when he took the outside berth with immediate success. Although small, he is very fast, centres with precision, and possesses excellent ball control. Undoubtedly he is a young man with a future." He was immediately popular with the Bloomfield Road faithful who repeatedly applauded his performance on the occasion of his home debut against Clapton Orient. Inspired by his sparkling display on the wing, Blackpool won 3-0, the victory taking Blackpool safe from having to apply for re-election. In the following season he shared the outside right berth with John Gow. He was subsequently transfer listed with a fee of £100 on his head, but an appeal to the Football League against the size of the fee saw Blackpool agree to a reduction to £25, but the FL Committee fixed it at £15, allowing the player to find a new club. Initially with Bristol City he played only twice and scored once in

the League side, but after a season in the Southern League with Exeter City he found more opportunities in his second spell at Ashton Gate with 41 appearances and five goals. By 1939 he was back in Exeter, working as a joint caretaker with his wife Florence and living at 7, Market Street.
Appearances: FL: 21 apps 1 gl Total: 21 apps 1 gl

COTTON, Thomas Arthur
Outside left
Born: Blackburn, 4th June 1879
Debut v Barnsley (a) 11.2.98, lost 1-2
CAREER: Skerton July 1896. **Blackpool December 1898.**

Blackpool's dismal record on the road – ten consecutive defeats - was not improved upon at Oakwell, despite the 1-2 defeat being an improvement in terms of goals conceded; previous thrashings included 0-7 at Gainsborough Trinity, 0-6 at Walsall and 1-6 at Burslem Port Vale. Blackpool had Cotton and Howson, from the Reserves, in place of Leadbeater and Birket, and the weakened attack rarely threatened the Barnsley goal. The local correspondent considered that "Fletcher, Blackpool's goalkeeper, gave one of the smartest displays that had been seen at Oakwell for a very long time."
Appearances: FL: 1 app 0 gls Total: 1 app 0 gls

COWIE, Stanley
Inside right 5' 7½" 11st 6lbs
Born: Sunderland, March 1890
Died: River Tyne, Dunston, August 1927
Debut v Leicester Fosse (h) 28.10.11, drawn 1-1
CAREER: 1st Battalion King's Liverpool Regiment. Herrington Swifts. **Blackpool May 1911.** Seaham Harbour August 1912. Sunderland Rovers May 1913. Exeter City July 1914. South Shields March 1915. Barry F.C. 1920 to 1927.

On joining Blackpool, Stanley Cowie, a 21 year-old inside forward, had recently served in the Army and had scored five goals in a Regimental Cup final. He was largely in reserve during his season with Blackpool, but a highlight came at Hyde Road, Manchester, when his goal against Crewe Alexandra in the FA Cup finally took Blackpool into round two, after two previous games against the Railwaymen had ended all square, the first replay at Bloomfield Road remaining tied at 2-2 after extra time. Cowie's subsequent career brought little success, but after the Great War he joined Barry F.C. and remained for seven seasons until his tragic death in August 1927 when his body was recovered from the river Tyne, with his hands and feet tied. "Suicide while of unsound mind" was the verdict reached at the Gateshead inquest on 19th August 1927. It was stated by his wife at the inquest that her husband had travelled to Sunderland to look for work. He had received no close season wages from Barry FC but was due to play in a practice match for them on 20th August. Evidence regarding the recovery of the body showed that the feet were tied tightly with string. The hands were also tied tightly with string, with six inches of slack between them. In the clothing was a sum of £6, a watch and chain, a medal bearing the Barry club's name, and a return ticket to Cardiff. An uncle confirmed that there was insanity on Cowie's father's side of the family, and that a cousin had committed suicide just a week ago, cutting his own throat.
Appearances: FL: 3 apps 0 gls FAC: 2 apps 1 gl Total: 5 apps 1 gl

COX, John 'Jack' Thomas

Winger
5' 9½" 12st 7lbs
Born: Liverpool, 21st December 1877
Died: Walton-on-Thames, Surrey, 11th November 1955
Debut v Gainsborough Trinity (a) 2.10.97, lost 1-4
CAREER: South Shore Standard. South Shore F.C. May 1896. **Blackpool May 1897**. Liverpool May 1898. **Blackpool player-manager August 1909 to 1911.**

Although not a local man, Jack Cox learned most of his football in Blackpool. An extremely fast goalscoring winger, his 12 goals in 17 League appearances in 1897-98 led to

his early departure to Liverpool. Initially fielded on the right wing, when switched to the left his game blossomed and he received his international honours. Cox was also a noted athlete who won numerous handicap races including the 100 yards footballer's race organised by Dundee F.C. in 1902. In later years he became a top bowler, winning the Talbot and Waterloo competition in 1925. After appearing in 327 League matches and scoring 72 goals his eleven-year career at Anfield ended when he returned to Blackpool as captain and later team-manager. In his second season he led Blackpool to their best prewar finish, 7th in Division Two in 1910-11. After retiring at the close of the 1911-12 season Jack Cox became a well-known commission agent in Blackpool. A younger brother, William James Cox was a wandering centre forward who appeared in Football League, Southern League, Scottish League and Lancashire Combination football with limited success. His best returns being 18 goals in 31 Scottish League matches for Dundee, and four in nine matches for Heart of Midlothian.
Appearances: FL: 83 apps 18 gls FAC: 5 apps 0 gls Total: 88 apps 18 gls
Honours: England international, 3 caps 1901-1903. FL representative, 3 apps. (Liverpool) FL Division One champions 1901 & 1906. FL Division Two champions 1905.

CREWDSON, Robert 'Bob'

Right full back
5' 9" 12st 7lbs
Born: Blackpool, 17th October 1882
Died: Blackpool, 12th November 1956
Debut v Bristol City (h) 19.11.04, lost 2-4
CAREER: Fleetwood Amateurs. Fleetwood Mechanics. **Blackpool August 1904 to 1913.**

A powerful defender with nine seasons of meritorious service to the club, Bob Crewdson began with Fleetwood Amateurs, whom he assisted to the championship of the Preston and District League. Initially in reserve at Bloomfield Road, he succeeded Bob Birket in his second season and remained first choice at right full back throughout the majority of the next six seasons. In 1909 he was appointed captain and received a benefit from the club. In season 1911-12 he was denied an 'ever present' season when he severely wrenched his back while erecting a large mast on the Blackpool promenade for Royal visit festivities in April 1912. Working as a joiner and boatbuilder he was employed by J. Armour & Sons (Fleetwood) and later was a hotel manager with his wife as manageress.
Note: His parents were John (a joiner) and Elizabeth Gallacher, and although he registered with the Football League on 23rd August 1904 as Robert Crewdson, he did not change his name by Deed Poll from Gallacher to Crewdson until 8th July 1912 (With thanks to my co-author Mike for unravelling the mystery)
Appearances: FL: 210 apps 0 gls FAC: 13 apps 0 gls Total: 223 apps 0 gls

CROSSTHWAITE, Herbert
Goalkeeper 5' 10" 12st 0 lbs
Born: Preston, 4th April 1887
Died: Erdington, Birmingham, 20th May1944
Debut v Gainsborough Trinity (a) 29.9.06, lost 0-2
CAREER: Preston Post Office. Preston Swifts. Preston North End 1905. **Blackpool amateur May 1906.** Fulham May 1907, fee £15. Exeter City May 1909. Birmingham December 1910 to 1915.

Herbert Crossthwaite made his first appearance for Preston North End Reserves in February 1906 at the age of 17. He was signed by Blackpool as cover for the more experienced, former Norwich City goalkeeper, Tom Wilcox, who missed only one first team match throughout the season. Moving on to Fulham, whom he accompanied on their Ostend & Belgium tour in May 1907, he appeared in only two League matches, but finally secured a first team place with Exeter City, missing only one match prior to his transfer to Birmingham. He had originally worked as a postman but on moving to Birmingham he joined the City Police Force in September 1910 and was promoted to sergeant in July 1917, and to Inspector in June 1925. He was awarded the King's Jubille Medal in in May 1935 and retired from the

Force in September of the same year. He was subsequently landlord of the Hare & Hounds public house in Birmingham. Herbert's cousin, Albert was an outside right who played for Stockport County (137 matches) and Stoke (30 matches).
Appearances: FL: 1 app 0 gls Total: 1 app 0 gls

DALE, George

Full back
5' 9"   11st 7lbs
Born: Kidsgrove, 11th August 1883
Died: Stoke-on-Trent, January quarter 1936
Debut v Leicester Fosse (a) 12.2.10, lost 2-3
CAREER: Kidsgrove Diamond. Goldenhill Wanderers January 1902. Kidsgrove Wellington August 1904. Talke United June 1905. Kidsgrove Wellington May 1906. **Blackpool October 1908**. Wellington Town August 1913. Butt Lane Star August 1914.

A talented full back whose chances at Bloomfield Road were limited by the presence of Bob Crewdson and Charlie Gladwin, George Dale nevertheless enjoyed a fair amount of League action, his best return being 14 appearances in 1911-12. He enlisted in the South Wales Borderers at Brecon in April 1915, but a long-standing injury to his back did not improve after a month's treatment at Pembroke Dock Military Hospital, leading to his discharge as unfit for military service in July of the same year. George Dale was a coalminer who married Annie Anchors in September 1908. They had five children, sadly three of them died before the age of one.
Appearances: FL: 40 apps 0 gls Total: 40 apps 0 gls

DARLINGTON, Edward 'Eddie'

Outside left
Born: Preston, 14th August 1880
Died: Heath Charnock Hospital, Chorley, 12th July 1958
Debut v Burton United (h) 2.9.05, won 2-0
CAREER: St Mark's (Preston). Broughton FC. Oswaldtwistle Rovers 1902. Chorley May 1904. **Blackpool June 1905.** Oswaldtwistle Rovers October 1906. Chorley September 1909 to 1910. Ormskirk September 1913.

Eddie Darlington was unfortunately injured at Burslem Port Vale – his fourth match in nine days at the start of season 1905-06. His position on the left wing was initially filled by Tom Bate, and later by the amateur, John Hollingsworth. After his lengthy spell on the sidelines, Darlington marked his return to action in the Reserves by scoring two goals in a 3-0 win against Skelmersdale United in early April, but he did not get another opportunity in the League side and returned to Lancashire Combination football. Various employments outside of the game included a spell as a labourer with a timber merchant, a stationery engine driver, and latterly a market gardener and groundsman to Sir Mark Hollins.
Appearances: FL: 4 apps 0 gls Total: 4 apps 0 gls

DAVIES, John 'Jack' Oscar
Outside left
Born: Liverpool, July quarter 1881
Debut v Barnsley (h) 12.9.03, lost 0-2
CAREER: St Helens Recreation May 1899. Liverpool August 1900. **Blackpool July 1903.**

When Blackpool's star amateur wingman, Harold Hardman, moved on to Everton in May 1903 it was acknowledged this his position at outside left would not be an easy one to fill. Jack Davies, who had been operating as understudy to Jack Cox (q.v.) at Liverpool, was thought capable but failed to impress on his debut and was not afforded a

second opportunity. In mid season Blackpool found a worthy replacement in Marshall McEwan, the Scottish junior international.
Appearances: FL: 1 app 0 gls Total: 1 app 0 gls

DAVIES, Septimus 'Sep'

Outside left
5' 8" 10st 8lbs
Born: Middlesbrough, 15th August 1888
Died: Cleveland, April quarter 1977
Debut v Bury (a) 4.1.13, drawn 1-1
CAREER: Eston United. **Blackpool May 1912.** Newburn September 1913.

Sep Davies left his job as a railway shunter to take up Blackpool's offer of a professional contract, but spent his season at Bloomfield Road in reserve ranks as Peter Quinn dominated the left wing berth. Davies' three League outing were made consecutively and in addition to his debut he appeared in a 1-1 home draw against Glossop and a 2-4 away defeat at Fulham. He returned to the North East in the close season, and his name was spotted many years later in 1939 when he was employed as a stocktaking clerk in a Steelworks.
Appearances: FL: 3 apps 0 gls Total: 3 apps 0 gls

DAWSON, Harold 'Harry'

Outside left
5' 8" 11st 0lbs
Born: Bolton, 14th December 1886
Died: Ashton-under-Lyne, January quarter 1951
Debut v Glossop (a) 20.3.09, lost 0-3
CAREER: Bolton St. Luke's. Padiham November 1904. Atherton Church House May 1905. Rossendale United May 1906. Everton April 1908. **Blackpool March 1909**. Croydon Common July 1911. West Ham United March 1912. Croydon Common June 1913. Southampton January 1917. Gillingham November 1919.

Harry Dawson's arrival at Blackpool came too late in the season to save the Seasiders from a re-election application, which, thankfully, was successful. A bright start to the following campaign included an opening day win at Manchester City, Dawson scoring the winning goal against the eventual champions of the Second Division. However, the return to Blackpool of England international wingman Jack Cox from Liverpool, effectively curtailed Dawson's involvement in the League side. On a happy note, he did find himself a bride in the town, marrying a Blackpool girl, Margaret Ward Gill on 12th September 1910.
Appearances: FL: 26 apps 4 gls FAC: 2 apps 0 gls Total: 28 apps 4 gls

DEWHURST, Arthur Wellesley
Goalkeeper
Born: Blackburn, 4th December 1873
Died: Mossley, 14th November 1919
Debut v Glossop (h) 31.12.1898, lost 1-2
CAREER: South Shore. Blackburn Rovers October 1894. **Blackpool December 1898.** Padiham April 1901. Haslingden September 1906. Padiham August 1907. Oswaldtwistle Rovers October 1907. Padiham September 1910.

Billed only as "Blackpool's latest amateur signing" in the local press, Arthur Dewhurst deputised for regular custodian Albert Fletcher at Glossop, his hurried recruitment triggered by the fact that outfield player Harry Stirzaker had been asked to keep goal in the previous match, a 0-5 defeat at Small Heath on Boxing Day. The New Year's Eve encounter against Glossop was played in atrocious conditions, rain falling in torrents throughout. It was the final match played at the Athletic Ground and visitors Glossop took the points, despite the best efforts of Dewhurst, who made a number of excellent saves.
Appearances: FL: 1 app 0 gls Total: 1 app 0 gls

DICKSON, James
Left half back
Born: Kirkham, July quarter 1876
Died: Lostock Hall, near Preston, 17th March 1938

Debut v Burton Swifts (a) 17.9.98, lost 1-3
CAREER: Blackpool July 1898. Kirkham FC August 1905. Shankhouse May 1908.

In the season when the Blackpool club migraited from the Athletic Ground to Raikes Hall, they also finished the season in 16th position in Division Two and failed to gain re-election. Apprentice blacksmith James Dickson was just one of seven players who made a single appearance during the dire campaign.
Appearances: FL: 1 app 0 gls Total: 1 app 0 gls

DIDYMUS, Edward John

Outside right
5' 7" 11st 4lbs
Born: Portsmouth, 13th April 1885
Died: France, 12th April 1918
Debut v Oldham Athletic (a) 11.12.09, lost 0-2
CAREER: Portsmouth January 1905. Northampton Town May 1907. Huddersfield Town October 1908. **Blackpool June 1909**. Burslem Port Vale November 1910.

Edward Didymus was a greengrocer's assistant from school and later a tramdriver with Portsmouth Corporation. A versative footballer, he appeared in six different positions for Portsmouth in one season and was leading scorer for the reserve team for two seasons. His first Football League club was Huddersfield Town, but he did not graduate to the senior side, his two appearances for Blackpool being his only involvement at League level. Moving on to Burslem Port Vale, he made his debut at centre forward against Congleton Town in a North Staffordshire & District League match in November 1910, but departed in the following month. He was back and living in Portsmouth when he enlisted as a Private in the Duke of Cambridge's Own (Middlesex Regiment). He lost his life in France in 1918 leaving a widow and four children.
Appearances: FL: 2 apps 0 gls Total: 2 apps 0 gls

DOLLIN, James William
Centre forward 6' 0" 13st 2lbs
Born: Hull, 29th June 1890
Debut v Gainsborough Trinity (a) 4.11.11, drawn 0-0
CAREER: Fleetwood. Burnley May 1909. Fleetwood August 1910. **Blackpool September 1911.** Fleetwood September 1913.

A Fleetwood fisherman and strapping central defender who appeared in eight League matches for Burnley before returning to Fleetwood after his single season at Turf Moor. Blackpool considered that Dollin's build and robust approach would be best utilised at centre forward, and he did succeed in Central League matches, on one occasion netting five goals. He was afforded more first team opportunities in 1912-13, but at inside right, the centre forward position shared equally beween George Wilson and Joe Bainbridge. Dollin scored his only League goal in the penultimate fixture of the season, a 2-1 victory against Huddersfield Town. During the Great War he served as a gunner in the RGA. In post war years he was a member of the Hesketh Grand Lodge of Freemasons from 1919. Twenty years later Census reports revealed that he was employed as a fish market supervisor. An unconfirmed report stated that he had died in Victoria, Australia, in 1971.
Appearances: FL: 18 apps 1 gl FAC: 2 apps 0 gls Total: 20 apps 1 gl

DONNELLY, Samuel 'Sam'

Inside right
5' 8" 11st 2lbs
Born: Annbank, Tarbolton, Ayrshire, 14th August 1873
Died: Ayr, 2nd June 1958
Debut v Lincoln City (a) 5.9.96, lost 1-3
CAREER: Annbank. Notts County July1893. **Blackpool June1896**. Annbank.

The small Ayrshire village of Annbank reared many talented footballers who subsequently found fame in professional ranks, Sam Donnelly being a typical example. Persevering, tricky and hardworking he showed marked improvement during his first

season with Notts County as he acclimatised to English football. He established a regular berth by mid season and crowned a term of genuine progress by collecting a FA Cup winners' medal for his appearance in the Goodison Park final against Bolton Wanderers. Sadly, his second second season ended prematurely when he sufferd a broken leg in a collision with a Newcastle defender in March 1895. He was out of football for over a year before joining Blackpool for their first season as a Football League club. His final outing came against Newcastle United on 16th January 1897, but whether it was injury (again) that curtailed his season was not revealed. Certainly to that point he had fully justified his place in the side, being excellent in combination and scoring some useful goals.
Appearances: FL: 14 apps 5 gls FAC: 4 apps 1 gl Total: 18 apps 6 gls
Honours: (Notts County) FA Cup winners 1894

DORRINGTON, Joseph 'Joe' Ralph

Goalkeeper
6' 2" 11st 8lbs
Born: Lichfield, Staffordshire, 8th January 1878
Died: Liverpool City, New South Wales, Australia, 5th January 1928
Debut v New Brighton Tower (a) 1.9.00, drawn 0-0
CAREER: Preston & District League football. Blackburn Rovers November 1897. **Blackpool January 1900, registered for FL matches July 1900**. Kettering cs 1903. **Blackpool re-registered July 1904, re-signed on amateur forms June 1905**. Colne A.F.C. September 1906. Oswaldtwistle Rovers November 1906. Birmingham April 1907. Shrewsbury Town November 1913.

An ideally built goalkeeper, Joe Dorrington began with Blackburn Rovers at the age of nineteen. Despite failing to graduate to League level at Ewood, he gave excellent service to Blackpool, initially in the Lancashire League as deputy for Griffiths the Welsh international. It was reported in March 1902 that while keeping goal he had played in more matches than he had conceded goals, and when Griffiths departed and Blackpool regained their position in Division Two of the Football League, Dorrington was handed the first team jersey and made maximum appearances in his first season, was rarely absent in his second, but then found increasing competition from Bill Wright and Arthur Hull in his third campaign. After a season away with Kettering Dorrington returned to Bloomfield Road but was operating in the Reserves when he was signed by Colne AFC, as cover for their injured goalkeeper, Stephen Tillotson (q.v.) who later joined Blackpool in May 1907. The son of a publican, Joe joined the Police Force and lived for a time in the Preston Police Station.
Appearances: FL: 78 apps 0 gls FAC: 9 apps 0 gls Total: 87 apps 0 gls

DOUGLAS, William

Goalkeeper
5' 9"
Born: Dundee, 26th October 1875
Died: Huron County, Ontario, Canada, 1958
Debut v Lincoln City (a) 5.9.96, lost 1-3
CAREER: Dundee Our Boys. Ardwick May 1890. Newton Heath January 1894. Derby County February 1896. **Blackpool June1896**. Warmley FC. June 1898. Wellingborough Town January 1899. Dundee August 1899. Dundee Wanderers August 1900.

William Douglas was initially recruited from Scotland by the Ardwick club (who later became Manchester City). He was ever-present in their first season in the Football Alliance, and missed only two matches in 1892-93 when Ardwick made their Football League debut in Division Two. He joined Newton Heath late in 1892-93, and from the start of the following season he played in 48 consecutive League matches before being suspended sine-die. This followed what was described as a "disgraceful beating" in the first round of the Manchester Cup by Fairfield, who won 5-2 at Clayton. Douglas was soon fixed up with Derby County but he did not stay there for very long. Joining

Blackpool for their debut in the Football League he was ever-present for two seasons. He next joined Warmley who failed to complete their Southern League programme in 1898-99, resigning after 17 games. Douglas then returned home to Dundee, spent a season at Dens Park in the Scottish League before transferring to Dundee Wanderers of the Northern League. In early days he worked as a coal salesman, later joining the Tay Division Royal Engineers (Volunteers) for five years as a piper. His attestation papers had him living at 256 Harvey Road, Toronto, Canada, as he joined the 128th Battalion Canadian Expeditionary Force. A later address for him was the Victor Inn, King Street, East Toronto.
Appearances: FL: 60 apps 0 gls FAC: 5 apps 0 gls Total: 65 apps 0 gls

DRAIN, Thomas 'Tommy'/ 'Digger'
Centre half back 5' 8½" 12st 10lbs
Born: Pollockshaws, 26th June 1879
Died: Edinburgh Royal Infirmary, 19th September 1952
Debut v Lincoln City (a) 9.10.09, drawn 2-2
CAREER: Drongan Juniors 1899. Glasgow Celtic 1900. Ayr United August 1901. Maybole 1902. Bradford City October 1903. Leeds City May 1905. Kilmarnock May 1906. Aberdeen June 1907. Vale of Leven (loan) October 1907. Carlisle United May 1907. Exeter City August 1908. Woolwich Arsenal May 1909. **Blackpool September 1909**. Nithsdale Wanderers October 1910. Galston FC September 1911.

Tommy 'Digger' Drain was born at Pollockshaws, one of ten children, and reared in the mining village of Drongan. It was here that he learned his football, and soon became the leading light in the Drongan Juniors team. Following a brilliant display in an Ayrshire Junior Cup final, he was approached by several clubs, and opted to join Glasgow Celtic. After just two months, however, he was transferred to Ayr United. His subsequent career did not lack variety on either side of the border, his best spell in League football coming with Bradford City (13 goals in 34 League and Cup matches). Joining Leeds City for their debut in The Second Division of the Football League, he scored twice in his second appearance, a 2-2 draw against Lincoln City, but failed to hold his place in the side, appearing in just nine League matches, in which he scored three goals. He had assisted six different clubs in the three years preceding his arrival at Blackpool, and by this time he was operating as a centre half back. With Jimmy Connor firmly established as pivot at Bloomfield Road, Drain spent most of his final League season in the Reserves. Tommy Drain lived in Fife from 1918 and was a Fife fireman.
Appearances: FL: 4 apps 0 gls Total: 4 apps 0 gls
Honours: Scottish Junior International.

DUCKWORTH, Thomas 'Tom' Crook D.C.M.

Outside right
5' 8" 11st 0lbs
Born: Whitebirk, 25th December 1880
Debut v Burslem Port Vale (a) 6.9.02, drawn 1-1
CAREER: Union Star (Blackpool). Anderson's Xl. Etrurians (Blackpool). Lytham F.C. 1901. **Blackpool April 1902**. West Ham United May 1903. Blackburn Rovers November 1903. **Blackpool June 1905 to May 1906**. Nelson November 1906. Hyde F.C November 1907. Oswaldtwistle Rovers July 1908. Blackpool Athletic September 1908. Darwen September 1912. Servette (Switzerland) coach 1921 to 1929. Switzerland national team coach 1924 and in the 1928 Olympic Games. Servette (Switzerland) 1930 to 1931. Lyon Olympique Universitaire (France) coach 1931-32 and again 1934. AS Saint-Etienne (France) coach 1934 to 1936. Lyon Olympique Villeurbanne (France) coach 1937 to 1938. Lyon Olympique Villeurbanne (france) coach 1945 to 1946.

Tom Duckworth, a local outside right, caught the committee's eye by displaying remarkably good form in Blackpool Medal Competition matches. Although he had lived in Blackpool for some time, he was not a Fylde lad, having been born at Whitebirk, near Blackburn. After playing with the Union Star at Blackpool, he joined Anderson's Xl, afterwards the Etrurians, playing alongside Swarbrick, of Blackburn Rovers, and Billy Anderton (q.v.)

of Blackpool. A season with Lytham preceded his transfer to Blackpool, and a promising first season in Division Two attracted the scouts. Sadly, a move to West Ham United brought no first team football, and he was similarly under employed with Blackburn Rovers, appearing in just one League match and one FA Cup-tie. A return to Blackpool saw him playing a splendid game at outside right, although much of his best work was not put to better use, his accurate centres rarely turned to account by his inside partners. A lengthy spell in the Lancashire Combination was interrupted by the outbreak of World War One. He was serving as a 2nd Lieutenant with the Liverpool Scottish Regiment when he was awarded the D.C.M. in October 1916 for carrying seven wounded soldiers to safety under circumstances of great peril. A lengthy and very successful career in coaching commenced in Switzerland, and followed in France at either side of the Second World War.
Appearances: FL: 28 apps 5 gls FAC: 2 apps 0 gls Total: 30 apps 5 gls

DUNKLEY, Albert Edward

Outside left
Born: Earls Barton, Northants, 29th July 1877
Died: Northampton, 15th January 1949
Debut v Barnsley (a) 1.9.06, lost 2-3
CAREER: Earls Barton Westleyans. Rushden Town September 1896. Northampton Town July 1897. Leicester Fosse May 1900. Northampton Town February 1901. New Brompton July 1901. Queens Park Rangers (trial) 1903. Blackburn Rovers August 1903. Bristol Rovers May 1904. **Blackpool August 1906**. Earls Barton September 1907. Northampton Town February 1908. St Michael's Thursday (Northampton) October 1911.

Recruited by Blackpool following two excellent seasons with Bristol Rovers (59 League and Cup matches and 10 goals), Albert Dunkley had assisted the Rovers to win the championship of the Southern League in 1904-05, and the Gloucester Cup in the same season. At Bloomfield Road he faced stiff competition for the left wing spot from Billy Anderton, each appearing in 18 matches during the season. Blackpool was his last League club, his modest career at this level amounting to 31 matches and four goals. At the time of his death he was working as a publican at The Old House & Home, Wellingborough Road, Northampton.
Appearances: FL: 17 apps 3 gls FAC: 1 app 0 gls Total: 18 apps 3 gls

EAVES, Richard
Outside right
Born: Poulton-le-Fylde
Debut v Grimsby Town (h) 18.2.99, lost 3-6
CAREER: **Blackpool February 1899, and re-signed October 1900. Again signed, as an amateur, August 1904.** Later noted with Brynn Central in January 1907.

All of Richard Eaves' five first team appearances came in the relegation season 1898-99 when he replaced local wingman James Banks, initially in four consecutive matches. On their travels, Blackpool had been leaking goals in alarming proportions, but on the occasion of Eaves debut against Grimsby Town, it was the first time that six goals had been conceded at home. As Blackpool returned to Division Two after spending one season in the Lancashire League, Richard Eaves was re-signed, but he did not get another opportunity at first team level.
Appearances: FL: 5 apps 0 gls Total: 5 apps 0 gls

ELMORE, George

Inside left
5' 8" 11st 7lbs
Born: Witton, Northwich, Cheshire, 3rd July 1880
Died: K.I.A., La Boisselle, Picardy, France, 1st July 1916
Debut v Manchester City (a) 2.9.09, won 2-1
CAREER: Witton Villa 1900. Witton Albion. Broadheath August 1902. Manchester United

(trial) December 1902. West Bromwich Albion January 1903. Bristol Rovers August 1903, fee £40. Witton Albion September 1904. Altrincham November 1904. Glossop October 1907. **Blackpool June 1909.** Partick Thistle August 1910. St Mirren 1912. Witton Albion August 1914. St Bernard's August 1915. Broxburn United October 1915.

Some four years after being released by West Bromwich Albion after just four first team matches, George Elmore had the satisfaction of scoring the winning goal for Glossop on his debut against his former colleagues in October 1907. After scoring 14 goals in 35 League appearances he was transferred to Blackpool, and continued his happy knack of scoring against former teammates, when he netted two at Glossop in a 3-2 win on 2nd April 1910. Leaving after just one season to join Partick Thistle, he had an excellent first season at Firhill, in all matches scoring 16 goals, including a hat trick in a 7-2 Scottish Cup win against St Bernard's. He was less successful in his second season, scoring six goals in 22 League matches. He did, however, collect a runners-up medal in the final of the Glasgow Cup, won by the Rangers at Celtic Park before an attendance of 58,000 spectators. Two seasons with St Mirren followed in which he scored 17 goals in 62 League matches, leaving Love Street following the Buddies relegation from the First Division in 1914. Two years later, George Elmore was killed in the First Word War while serving as a lance corporal in the 15th Battalion of the Royal Scots Regiment.
Appearances: FL: 34 apps 6 gls Total: 34 apps 6 gls

ELSTON, Henry
Winger 5' 8"
Born: Blackpool, 3rd April 1878
Died: Allegheny County, Pennsylvania, USA, 1st July 1960
Debut v Grimsby Town (h) 18.2.99, lost 3-6
CAREER: Blackpool January 1899.

Local wingman Henry Elston, along with Richard Eaves, was given his first opportunity in the League side against Grimsby Town at Raikes Hall. Elston's only other outing had been in a friendly match against South Shore, and it was a bold move by the Blackpool directors to introduce two wingmen with no experience in senior football. On the day, the new look forward line managed to score three goals, but Grimsby Town scored six, and Blackpool's sorry season continued in similar vein, ending in relegation from Division Two. The son of a joiner, Henry married Helena Wilson and they emigrated to the USA on 28th August 1912, and were naturalized 1st April 1918. In 1917 he was working for Huntley Manufacturing Company as a Millwright carpenter in Silver Creek USA.
Appearances: FL: 4 apps 0 gls Total: 4 apps 0 gls

EVANS, Arthur Thomas
Half back 5' 10½" 11st 8lbs
Born: Horwich, Bolton, January quarter 1884
Died: Killed in action on the Somme, 31st July 1916, age 32
Debut v Hull City (a) 30.10.09, won 2-1
CAREER: Mawdsley (Bolton). Manchester City May 1906. Distillery July to September 1907. Rossendale United November 1907. **Blackpool July 1909.** Manchester City June 1912. Exeter City June 1913.

Despite being twice signed by Manchester City, Arthur Evans was not given a first team opportunity. He joined Blackpool from Rossendale United as a centre half back but after spending almost all of his first season in the Reserves, a switch to right half back afforded him more opportunities as Jimmy Connor remained the automatic selection at centre half. A return to Manchester City preceded a final move to Exeter City, but he appeared in only six Southern League matches for the Grecians. Arthur Evans lost his life while serving as a sergeant with the 24th Royal Fusiliers in France, he was just 32 years old.
Appearances: FL: 37 apps 0 gls Total: 37 apps 0 gls

EVANS, Lorenzo

Outside left
5' 8½" 11st 0lbs
Born: Newton Heath, 6th March 1878
Died: Poulton-le-Fylde, 6th February 1945, age 66
Debut v New Brighton Tower (a) 1.9.00, drawn 0-0
CAREER: Newton Heath Athletic. Manchester Grammar School September 1890 to July 1895. St Anne's Rovers. St Anne's Amateurs. Blackburn Rovers amateur September 1898. Glossop amateur July 1899. **Blackpool amateur August 1900 to May 1903.**

A reserve wingman with Blackburn Rovers with just two first team appearances, Lorenzo Evans found more opportunities on joining Glossop for their debut in the First Division of the Football League. Handily versatile, he appeared on both wings, and made odd starts as centre forward and inside left. He moved on after Glossop's relegation from the top flight and next joined Blackpool, for whom he made 54 League appearances and scored six goals. He was an architect and surveyor by profession.
Appearances: FL: 54 apps 6 gls FAC: 4 apps 2 gls Total: 58 apps 8 gls

FISKE, William 'Bill'

Goalkeeper
Born: Beccles, Suffolk 7th August 1885
Died: K.I.A. Marne, France, 27th May 1918
Debut v Burnley (a) 25.12.07, lost 1-2
CAREER: Bungay FC. Beccles F.C. Suffolk County 1905. Bungay F.C. Norwich City October 1906. **Blackpool May 1907**. Nottingham Forest May 1914, fee £250.

Bill Fiske began as an inside forward until he took over from an injured goalkeeper and found his true niche. He enlisted in the Norfolk Regiment in August 1903 and in 1905 while serving in South Africa represented an Army eleven against the Corinthians. After about half a season with Norwich City Fiske moved to Blackpool. An ideally built goalkeeper, he proved wonderfully consistent throughout his seven seasons, agility and courage being the principal features of his play. In March 1913 the Blackpool directors gave him a benefit match and presented him with a gold watch. However, after differing with the Seasiders on the question of terms, he was placed on the transfer list, and he cost Nottingham Forest £250, the fee fixed by the Football League Management Committee. In the previous season, Forest had conceded 76 goals and finished 20th in Division Two, the lowest point in their history. Fiske's signing was expected to bring some much- needed efficiency in goal. In the event, he enlisted in the army on 21st August 1914, before Forest's season had kicked off. He was on leave from France when he made his five appearances, commencing with a Christmas Day debut at the City Ground. He was later killed on the Marne near the village of Fismes during the German spring offensive. He was seen going over the top in his shirtsleeves and his body was never found. He is commemorated on the Soissons Memorial.
Appearances: FL: 212 apps 0 gls FAC: 9 apps 0 gls Total: 221 apps 0 gls

FLETCHER, Albert Edward
Goalkeeper 6' 3"
Born: Coseley, Staffordshire January quarter 1878
Debut v Glossop (a) 3.9.98, lost 1-4
CAREER: Blackpool March 1898. West Bromwich Albion May 1900.

At 6 feet 3 inches and with a build to match, Albert Fletcher presented a formidable barrier to any onrushing forward. He was first fielded in a friendly match arranged by the Blackpool directors to give trials to five promising juniors and his display won him the opportunity to follow William Douglas, Blackpool's ever-present goalkeeper in the two previous seasons. Often described as "Blackpool's best player" despite operating

behind a decidedly leaky defence, he missed just two matches over the Christmas holiday period in which one goal was scored and seven conceded. After a season in the Lancashire League Blackpool resumed in Division Two in 1900-01 with Joe Dorrington in goal. Albert Fletcher, meanwhile, had signed for West Bromwich Albion but did not get a first team opportunity in a season when Albion finished at the bottom of the First Division and were relegated.
Appearances: FL: 32 apps 0 gls FAC: 2 apps 0 gls Total: 34 apps 0 gls

FOSTER, John 'Jack' Samuel
Inside/Centre forward 5' 7"
Born: Parkgate, near Rotherham, 19th November 1877
Died: Huddersfield, 5th February 1946
Debut v Bristol City (h) 7.9.01, lost 0-2
CAREER: Rotherham Church Institute. Thornhill United May 1900. **Blackpool May 1901.** Rotherham Town May 1902. Watford May 1905. Sunderland December 1907, fee £800. West Ham United May 1908. Southampton March 1909, in exchange for F. Costello. Huddersfield Town May 1909. Castleford Town July 1910. Morley F.C. August 1911. Huddersfield Town assistant trainer August 1912, later assistant manager. Bradford City assistant manager August 1926, caretaker manager January 1928. Portsmouth scout October 1937.

Discovered, quite by accident, by Blackpool's secretary, Mr Tom Barcroft, when travelling to watch a match at the Gainsborough Trinity club, Jack Foster, an effective opportunist, appeared in all five forward positions for Blackpool before embarking on a wandering and largely successful career. He cost Sunderland £800 – a fortune at that time, after he has scored 12 goals in 13 Southern League appearances for Watford in 1907-08. Sadly, Jack's health deteriorated, and medical advice suggested a return to the south, hence his move to West Ham United after only six months at Roker Park. Could it have been that his employment outside of the game, that of a self-employed chimney sweep, did not mix well with life as a professional footballer! He was raised in a family of 15 children – seven sons and eight daughters.

Appearances: FL: 28 apps 6 gls FAC: 3 apps 0 gls Total: 31 apps 6 gls

FRANCIS, Ernest 'Ernie'

Centre forward
Born: King's Norton, 1st April 1886
Died: Stirchley, Birmingham, 6th February 1954
Debut v Bradford City (a) 28.10.05, lost 1-2
CAREER: Aston Villa November 1904. **Blackpool amateur July, professional August 1905.** Aston Villa November 1907. Worcester City February 1908. Walsall August 1908. Worcester City August 1909.Wolverhampton Wanderers May 1913. Worcester City May 1914. Bournville Athletic March 1915.

Ernie Francis was first tried by Blackpool when two regular forwards were on the injured list but after two matches he was returned to reserve ranks. Given a second opportunity in January, his goal against Crystal Palace at Villa Park finally took Blackpool into round two of the FA Cup, after two previous meetings between the sides had ended all square. Aston Villa was Francis' next port of call, but he did not feature in the first team who finished the season as runners-up to Manchester United for the First Division championship. The first of his three separate spells with Worcester City followed and between spells with Walsall and Wolverhampton Wanderers he scored 96 goals in 144 appearances for the Birmingham League club.
Appearances: FL: 38 apps 11 gls FAC: 6 apps 1 gl Total: 44 apps 12 gls

GAMBLE, George Frederick
Inside right
Born: Belgrave, Leicester, 24th October 1877
Died: Leicester 27th July 1949
Debut v Small Heath (h) 8.3.99, drawn 1-1
CAREER: Leicester Fosse November 1897. Stalybridge Rovers May 1898. **Blackpool February1899.** Millwall May 1899. Newton Heath October 1900. Barnsley January 1901.

Newton Heath October 1901. Hall's Collieries November 1902. Fulham October 1904.

In Blackpool's relegation season, 1898-99, George Gamble's five League appearances resulted in one win, one defeat and three draws. He scored twice against Barnsley in a 3-1 home win on March 15th, and in his final appearance one week later, scored Blackpool's goal in a 1-1 draw against Woolwich Arsenal, some recompense for the 6-0 defeat against the same opponents just four days earlier. Gamble was better known as a cricketer, at various times assisting Leicestershire Second XI, London County and Surrey, for whom he appeared in eight first class matches in 1906 as a slow left-arm bowler and lower order right-hand batsman. He took 26 wickets at 26.57 with a best performance of five wickets for 78 runs. Originally employed as a clicker in the local shoe industry, he was later a clerk and in 1939 a landscape gardener.
Appearances: FL: 5 apps 3 gls Total: 5 apps 3 gls

GASKELL, Herbert Ralph
Full back
Born: Gorton, Manchester, 14th March 1884
Died: Sale, Cheshire, 5th May 1938
Debut v Chelsea (a) 22.4.12, lost 1-4
CAREER: **Blackpool amateur March 1912**

Signed as cover for the full back position, Herbert Gaskell was accompanied by his younger brother, Arthur, who had earlier assisted Bolton Wanderers in 102 League matches (two goals) between 1905-09, and was with Macclesfield from November 1911, prior to joining his brother at Bloomfield Road. Herbert, who was a commercial traveller in roof glazing, made a solitary League appearance while brother Arthur did not get an opportunity with Jimmy Jones and Bob Crewdson the well established regular pairing in the back division.
Appearances: FL: 1 app 0 gls Total: 1 app 0 gls

GILLETT, George
Inside/centre forward
Born: Lytham, 6th October 1872
Died: Lytham, 4th November 1933
Debut v Glossop (a) 5.10.1901, lost 1-3
CAREER: Blackpool 21st August 1901.

Elder brother of Nicholas (q.v.), George Gillett was a late starter in senior football, being one day short of his 29th birthday when he made his League debut at Glossop. Three of his six first team appearances were all against Southport Central in the FA Cup, two goalless encounters being followed by a 1-2 defeat, after extra time, at Deepdale, Preston. George was a painter & decorator by trade.
Appearances: FL: 3 apps 0 gls FAC: 3 apps 0 gls Total: 6 apps 0 gls

GILLETT, Nicholas
Outside right
Born: Lytham, July quarter 1874
Died: Fylde, January quarter1920
Debut v Darwen FAC 3Q (a) 15.12.96, won 2-1
CAREER: **Blackpool May 1895, registered for FL matches June1896.**

Nicholas Gillett, with a season's experience as a Blackpool player before they entered the Football League, found few opportunities of first team football in 1896-97 with John Clarkin, the former Newton Heath forward, a fixture on the right wing. Nicholas, who earned his living as a plumber, was brother to George (q.v.)
Appearances: FL: 2 apps 0 gls FAC: 1 app 0 gls Total: 3 apps 0 gls

GILLIBRAND, Charles Sydney
Outside right
Born: Preston, 3rd January 1881
Died: Amounderness, January quarter 1958
Debut v Hastings & St Leonards, FAC 1 (h) won 2-0
CAREER: Longridge. Preston North End November 1907. **Blackpool September 1908**. Barrow February 1910.

One of a family of ten children, Charles Gillibrand first worked as a cart driver, and from 1911 to retirement was employed as a window cleaner. As a footballer he scored two goals in just three Division One matches for Preston North End, but then spent his Blackpool spell in reserve apart from one FA Cup-tie against modest opponents Hastings & St Leonards in which goals by Arthur Whalley and Eddie Threlfall took Blackpool through to round two and sterner opponents, Newcastle United. The Magpies went on to reach the semi-final and finish as champions of

Division One with a seven-point margin over runners-up, Everton. Blackpool, meanwhile, finished at the foot of Division Two, but their plucky display at St James' Park in round two of the Cup was widely praised. Perhaps performing before an attendance of 32,137 had inspired them!
Appearances: FAC: 1 app 0 gls Total: 1 app 0 gls

GILLOW, Wilfred 'Wilf' Bernard
Inside left 5' 8½" 10st 7lbs
Born: Preston, 8th July 1892
Died: County Durham Hospital, 12th March 1944
Debut v Barnsley (a) 12.10.12, lost 0-1
CAREER: Lancaster 1907. Preston North End 1910. Fleetwood September 1911. **Blackpool October 1912**. Preston North End September 1914. Seaforth Highlanders. (Wartime with Preston North End and Partick Thistle). Grimsby Town February 1920. Lancaster Town June 1922. Grimsby Town May 1923; appointed player-manager June 1924, and subsequently as manager only until April 1932. Middlesbrough manager March 1934 to his death.

A former schoolmate of George Wilson (q.v.) Wilf Gillow made his Football League debut as a 20 year old inside forward with Blackpool. With only ten and a half stones to throw into the fray he lacked any physical advantage, but he excelled as a clever forager and a provider rather than a goalscorer. A return to Preston North End brought only seven League appearances, but after the Great War he served Grimsby Town with distinction, firstly as a player (103 League appearances and five goals) and subsequently as manager, leading the Mariners from the Third to the First Division.
As a cricketer he played for Cleethorpes, Middlesbrough, Lancashire County Ground Staff and Lincolnshire. A personal highlight came when he appeared on the cricket field as a substitute for England versus Australia at Old Trafford while a member of the Lancashire CCC ground staff.
Appearances: FL: 26 apps 3 gls FAC: 2 apps 0 gls Total: 28 apps 3 gls
Honours: (Grimsby Town) FL Division Two runners-up 1929. FL Division Three North Champions 1926.

GITTINS, Alfred

Centre/Inside forward
5' 9" 11st 2lbs
Born: Manchester, 22nd February 1885
Died: Blackpool, 24th January 1960
Debut v West Bromwich Albion (h) 17.9.04, drawn 0-0
CAREER: Adlington. **Blackpool March 1902.** Atherton Church House May 1905. Luton Town May 1906. Queens Park Rangers May 1907. Aston Villa October 1908. Croydon Common May 1909. Fulham August 1910. Portsmouth December 1910. Accrington Stanley August 1911. Barrow January 1912. Partick Thistle June 1912. Dumbarton April 1914. Clydebank May 1916. Johnstone August 1917. Vale of Leven August 1918. King's Park September 1919. Clackmannan August 1921. Stenhousemuir September 1922. Dunkeld & Birnam 1923.

Although Alf Gittins appeared in just two Football League matches (one for Blackpool and one for Aston Villa) his overall career record was far more impressive, amounting to 45 goals in 181 matches for eight different clubs, spanning Football League, Scottish League and Southern League football. His best spells coming with Queens Park Rangers (42 Southern League matches and 17 goals) and Dumbarton (51 Scottish League matches and ten goals). Off the field, he was working as a junior articled clerk in 1901, but at the time of his marriage in 1925 he was working as an oxy acetylene welder. Along with his wife, a spell in the USA included work as an agriculturist in Brighton, Massachusetts, and later with a company named Budd Wheel, a car manufacturer based in Detroit.
Appearances: FL: 1 app 0 gls Total: 1 app 0 gls

GLADWIN, Charles 'Charlie' Edward

Full back 5' 11½" 12st 6lbs
Born: Worksop, 11th December 1887
Died: Rotherham, April quarter 1952
Debut v Gainsborough Trinity (h) 12.12.08, won 3-0
CAREER: Dinnington Main Colliery October 1907. **Blackpool December 1908, fee £15.** Sunderland October 1912, fee £1,200. Watford August 1919, appointed club trainer January to May 1920.

When Charlie Gladwin was transferred to Sunderland in October 1912, Blackpool received their biggest ever fee for the strapping full back who had cost just £15 some four years earlier. He played mainly in the Reserves upon arrival at Bloomfield Road but improved to a great extent, prompting one observer to comment: "His fearless tackling and vitality were a major influence on the side. He used his awesome physique to full advantage, dominating the whole penalty area and giving the wing halves freedom to attack." The one blot on his Blackpool record was a lengthy suspension by the FA following his being sent off for "Using and persisting in objectionable language to the referee in the match between Derby County and Blackpool at Derby on 24th February 1912." He missed the last nine matches of the season as a consequence. His transfer to Sunderland came in October of the following season and his performances, along with those by new goalkeeper Joe Butler from Glossop FC, took Sunderland to the League title. They were unfortunate to miss out on the 'Double' losing to Aston Villa in the final at Crystal Palace.
Appearances: FL: 87 apps 0 gls FAC: 6 apps 0 gls Total: 93 apps 0 gls
Honours: (Sunderland) FL champions 1913. FA Cup finalist 1913.

GOLDING, Percy Albert
Left full back 5' 7½" 11st 7lbs
Born: Mardy, South Wales, 5th November 1883
Died: Cardiff, 12th July 1961
Debut v West Bromwich Albion (h) 4.12.09, won 2-1
CAREER: Blackpool May 1909.

A capable reserve defender, able to occupy either flank, Percy Golding was on the small side for his position but one who found a fair amount of first team action in his first season. In 1910-11 he was restricted to just two appearances, with Crewdson and Gladwin the favoured pairing at full back.
Appearances: FL: 14 apps 0 gls FAC: 1 app 0 gls Total: 15 apps 0 gls

GOSLING, George
Centre half back
Born: Levenshulme, 7th August 1870
Died: Blackpool, 18th November 1933
Debut v Burslem Port Vale (h) 24.9.98, lost 0-4
CAREER: Blackpool 1896. First registered by FL 9th September 1898.

The son of a bookkeeper, George Gosling was first noted as captain of the Reserves who opened their 1896-97 Lancashire Combination season at Preston North End, as the first team travelled to Lincoln City to contest their first Football League fixture. Gosling's solitary first team appearance at the Athletic Ground was the fourth defeat in as many matches in the first month of season 1898-99 in which Blackpool were subsequently relegated from Division Two. George Gosling was living in Cambridge Road, Blackpool in 1901 and was employed by the Fylde Water Board as a water rate collector. **Note**: It seemed worth recording that one G. Gosling (Blackpool) was included in a listing of referees appointed by the Lancashire Combination in June 1913. It is thought likely that this would be the above George Gosling.
Appearances: FL: 1 app 0 gls Total: 1 app 0 gls

GOW, John

Forward
5' 5½"   10st 10lbs
Born: Liverpool, 26th March 1882
Died: February 1966
Debut v Glossop (a) 1.4.05, drawn 0-0
CAREER: Dominion Stevedores (Liverpool). **Blackpool March 1905**. Nelson June 1908.

There were probably very few Football League players who had taken part in a game of football in China, but this what John Gow, the Blackpool outside right, had done. He was serving on board one of H.M. battleships on the China station, and the team with which he played won the China Station Cup in 1902-03. Gow joined the Navy at the age of 16, but returning from abroad he bought himself out about 18 months later. He then joined Dominian Stevedores, from which club he joined Blackpool in March 1905. He was so successful in the few remaining matches of the season that he was re-signed for the following campaign in which a family bereavement caused him to be unavailable for the English Cup-tie against Sheffield United. Later in the same month he was injured in the early stages of the Third Round tie at Newcastle United and did not play again that season. He was greatly missed, but happily was able to resume for the following two seasons before he left to join Nelson, at about the same time he re-enrolled in the Navy as a leading seaman. Later again he worked as a yard foreman on Salford Docks.
Appearances: FL: 63 apps 4 gls FAC: 6 apps 0 gls Total: 69 apps 4 gls

GREEN, Benjamin 'Benny' Haigh

Inside forward
5' 7½"   12st 0lbs
Born: Barnsley, 23rd February 1882
Died: K.I.A. Arras, France, 26th April 1917
Debut v Wolverhampton Wanderers (a) 26.12.13, lost 0-1
CAREER: Pennistone United. Barnsley October 1901. Small Heath/Birmingham October 1903, fee £500. Burnley September 1909. Preston North End May 1911. **Blackpool December 1913 to 1915.**

Benny Green, a small but sturdy inside forward, was a seasoned performer who added useful experience to Blackpool's attack for a season and a half before League football was suspended for the duration of World War One. His football career commenced with Barnsley, for whom he scored 18 goals in 45 League matches. A lengthy spell with Small Heath (who subsequently became Birmingham F.C.) spanned 185 appearances and 45 goals. Along the way, he was the first to score a goal at the new St Andrews ground, and was presented with a piano to mark the occasion! Two seasons with Burnley brought 29 goals in 71 matches, and a similar record with Preston North End (73 matches and 23 goals) included 13 in 1912-13 when North End won the Second Division championship. On 12th June 1917 news was received in Blackpool that Benny Green was wounded and missing. He had enlisted in the King's Own Royal Lancaster Regiment from Blackpool in July 1915, and was shipped out to France at the end of the year. He had actually gone missing and believed killed on 26th April 1917, and his body was never found.
Appearances: FL: 31 apps 4 gls FAC: 2 apps 0 gls 33 apps 4 gls
Honours: (Preston North End) FL Division Two champions 1913

GREENHALGH, Peter
Left full back
Debut v Blackburn Park Road, FAC 3Q (a) won 1-0
CAREER: Horwich. **Blackpool May 1900.** Haydock August 1901. Rochdale Town July 1902. Rossendale United August 1903. Oldham Athletic June 1904. Walkden Central September 1905. Newton Heath Athletic March 1906, and re-signed July 1906.

As deputy to Bob Birket for the left full back position Peter Greenhalgh found few opportunities as Blackpool returned to Division Two in 1900-01. A series of rapid moves eventually took him to Oldham Athletic whom he assisted to promotion from Division Two of the Lancashire Combination, despite an early observation that he appeared overweight on arrival at Hudson Fold, he appeared in most matches during the successful campaign
Appearances: FL 1 app 0 gls FAC: 2 apps 0 gls Total: 3 app 0 gls

GREGSON, William 'Bill' Cameron Smart
Inside left 5' 7" 10st 7lbs
Born: Berwick-upon-Tweed, 8th March 1890
Died: Taunton, Somerset, 13th January 1977
Debut v Derby County (h) 6.3.15, won 2-1
CAREER: Berwick Grammar School. Durham University. Berwick Rangers. Stockton November 1912. **Blackpool amateur March 1915**. Sunderland amateur 1920. Hartlepools United 1921. Chilton Colliery Recreation Athletic. Kelloe. Trimdon Grange Colliery.

After just two matches in the Central League side Bill Gregson was handed his Football League debut against the League leaders, Derby County, and finished on the winning side. Described, by one observer as: "A hard worker who needs to cultivate more speed". Two months prior to his debut he had enlisted as a Subaltern, and was commissioned in July as a 2nd Lieutenant in the 7th Northumberland Fusiliers. A member of the scholastic profession, initially house and games master at Laxton Grammar School, he retired after 38 years in September 1955. An all-round sportsman, Gregson played cricket for Berwick Grammar School, Berwick C.C., Berwickshire, Durham University and Morpeth. In August 1921 he took 6 wickets for 27 runs and 6 for 29 for Berwick against Berwickshire.
Appearances: FL: 3 apps 0 gls Total: 3 apps 0 gls

GRUNDY, James
Centre forward
Born: Astley Bridge
Debut v Grimsby Town (a) 19.3.98, lost 0-3
CAREER: Blackpool February 1898.

On 26th February 1898, the 'Lancashire Evening Post' reported: "Grundy, the last forward signed, is to be given another chance. It was unfair to judge him from his display in the friendly match against South Shore, and when he gets a little more self-confidence, he may be seen in a different light altogether." His chance came, as deputy for Bob Birket, but he appeared unready for League football and his outing at Grimsby Town proved to be the extent of his Football League acquaintance.
Appearances: FL: 1 app 0 gls Total: 1 app 0 gls

GRUNDY, William Alfred
Centre forward 5' 7½" 10st 1lb
Born: Manchester, 12th September 1886
Died: Southport, 27th September 1957
Debut v West Bromwich Albion (h) 10.11.06, won 2-1 (scored one goal)
CAREER: An amateur throughout with **Blackpool April 1906**. Bolton Wanderers June 1908. **Blackpool again November 1908**. Northern Nomads. Huddersfield Town November 1909. Northern Nomads. **Blackpool again August 1911**. Port Vale.

A nimble, slightly built centre forward who elected to remain in the unpaid ranks throughout his football career while following his employment in the family business as a commercial traveller in drapery. Although briefly associated with another Football League club, Bolton Wanderers, Grundy earned a reputation in Division Two football and was a consistent scorer in three seasons at Bloomfield Road, the best of which, 1907-08, brought 13 goals in 26 League and Cup matches. It also included the season's only hat trick in a 4-3 victory against Lincoln City on 7th December 1907.

Appearances: FL: 59 apps 28 gls FAC: 2 apps 1 gl Total: 61 apps 29 gls

HALSALL, Lawrence 'Lollie'
Winger
Born: Ormskirk, January quarter 1872
Died: Ormskirk, February 1919, age 47
Debut v Burnley (a) 4.9.97, lost 1-5
CAREER: North Meols FC. Southport Central (debut) September 1891. North Meols FC 1893. Southport Central May 1895. **Blackpool May 1897**. Preston North End October 1897. Southport Central August 1900 to April 1901.

In three separate spells with Southport Central 'Lollie' Halsall appeared in 188 League and Cup matches, scoring 70 goals. When signed by Blackpool he was described as: "A skilfull outside left, wonderfully expert in ball control and centring, but rather lacking in weight." His stay at the Athletic Ground was brief and unrewarding, his five League outings taking in three different positions, commencing at outside left, followed by two at Inside left and two at centre forward. At this point he was probably pleased to join Preston North End for whom he scored two goals in his first four appearances. It was not until the final fixture of the season that North End retained their First Division status by a whisker – the bottom five clubs all finishing the season with 24 points. An injury at Bury in October 1899 brought a premature end to his spell at Deepdale after 54 League appearances and six goals. In March 1906 it was reported that Lollie Halsall was confined in Southport Infirmary suffering with a diseased bone in his foot. Sadly the foot had to be amputated and sympathy came from many friends and former colleagues. The Preston North End club granted him £10 and a collection was also made in a game against Bolton Wanderers. The Southport Central club also arranged for a collection to be made during the progress of a suitable match. The Promenade Bowling Club subscribed 23 shillings and YMCA and Park Villa held benefit matches for him.
Appearances: FL: 5 apps 1 gl Total: 5 apps 1 gl

HANCOCK, Harry Bentley

Inside-forward
5' 8" 11st 8lbs
Born: Tranmere, 1874. (Christened 18th November)
Died: Birkenhead, 8th August 1923
Debut v Burton United (h) 2.9.05, won 2-0
CAREER: Rock Ferry F.C. Melrose F.C. September 1892. Tranmere Rovers trial October 1902. Melrose F.C. November 1902. Port Sunlight May 1903. Stockport County *circa* February/March 1905. **Blackpool May 1905**. Oldham Athletic May 1906. Manchester City May 1908. West Bromwich Albion February 1909. Brierley Hill Alliance April 1910, retired due to injury in 1912.

Blackpool were intending to have a completely new forward line for season 1905-06, and the first to be signed was Harry Hancock of Stockport County, who had played in 16 matches in the previous season. After a quiet start at Bloomfield Road he opened his scoring account against his former colleagues, Stockport County, in a 2-0 win on 14th October. It was in the FA Cup, however, that his name became known to a wider audience, the 'Sheffield Evening Telegraph' reporting in February 1906 as follows: "Since Blackpool's return from Sheffield, Hancock, the light, nippy, elastic forward who scored both of Blackpool's goals inside the opening four minutes of the second half, has been lionised. Not only has he been frequently stopped on the street and congratulated by many admirers, he has received quite a number of presents, and a special one from the club. Hancock is the ex-Stockport County centre forward who came out with Rock Ferry, a small Cheshire team. A brother of his now plays for Stockport County." His two goals took Blackpool through to round three, at the expense of their First Division opponents, but the Cup run ended at Newcastle United before a crowd of 34,405 spectators, the Magpies going on to reach the Final at Crystal Palace where they lost 1-0 to

Everton. Moving on to Oldham Athletic Harry Hancock scored 23 of the team's 105 goals in Lancashire Combination matches and six in eight FA Cup ties. In the following season, as the Latics began their adventure as a Football League club, Hancock remained a fixture at inside-left until a serious ankle injury sidelined him for some two months from February 1908. Athletic narrowly missing out on promotion at the first attempt, finishing third in Division Two. A move to Manchester City brought no first team appearances, and just two League outings with West Bromwich Albion wound up his senior career. Outside of the game Harry Hancock worked as a cotton salesman, and was later a cotton broker.
Appearances: FL: 29 apps 6 gls FAC: 5 apps 3 gls Total: 34 apps 9 gls
Honours: (Oldham Athletic) Lancashire Combination Division 1 champions 1907.

HARDMAN , Harold Payne

Winger
5' 6½" 10st 4lbs
Born: Kirkmanshulme, Manchester, 4th April 1882
Died: Sale, Cheshire, 9th June 1965
Debut v Gainsborough Trinity (h) 8.9.00, drawn 1-1
CAREER: South Shore High School. South Shore Choristers. An amateur throughout with **Blackpool July 1900**. Everton May 1903. Manchester United August 1908. Bradford City January 1909. Stoke February 1910. Manchester United again September 1913. (Throughout his career with the mentioned clubs, Hardman was in addition a regular performer with Northern Nomads.)

Born in Manchester but brought up in Blackpool, at only eighteen years when he made his debut, Blackpool's tricky little winger Harold Hardman must have been one of the youngest League footballers of his day. He gained his first experience with the South Shore High School, with whom he spent five years. He first played at left half, then going forward to the wing, a position that he occupied with outstanding success. Not only successful as a footballer, Hardman also won laurels on the running track, winning the school championship on four occasions. On joining South Shore Choristers, he assisted them to reach the final of the Blackpool Medals Competition, won by Poulton. At this point he was invited by the Blackpool officials to sign an amateur form. He quickly became a regular on the left wing, delighting everyone with his ability. His successful debut in League football greatly pleasing his father, a Manchester solicitor, and his former schoolmates and schoolmasters. At the age of 21 the Blackpool club presented him with a gold watch in recognition of his services. While still studying law and residing in Blackpool, he was invited to join Everton. He played his first game for Everton Reserves against Liverpool Reserves, an evening match that drew a crowd of 30,000 spectators. Everton won 3-0 and Hardman was soon promoted into the first eleven. He was in the Everton team that won the FA Cup against Newcastle United in 1906, and was at the Crystal Palace again the following year when Sheffield Wednesday beat Everton in the final by 2-1. In addition to his two Cup Final appearances, Hardman played four times for England, scoring the winning goal against Ireland in 1907. An England Amateur international on numerous occasions, he won a gold medal in the 1908 Olympic Games when he helped England to beat Denmark at White City, London, by 2-0. Manchester United signed him in August 1908, but owing to the brilliance of England international outside left George Wall, he played only four times, and moved on to Bradford City in search of more regular football. Harold Hardman eventually returned to Manchester United and served the club faithfully for over fifty years as a director and fourteen years as chairman (1951-65). He additionally served the FA, the Lancashire FA and the Central League. A Manchester solicitor in 1908, he died at Sale aged 83 in June 1965.
Appearances: FL: 73 apps 10 gls FAC: 6 apps 1 gl Total: 79 apps 11 gls
Honours: England International, 4 caps, 1905-08. England Amateur International, 10 caps. FL representative, 1 app. (Everton) FA Cup winner 1906; finalist 1907.

HARRISON, Fred
Left half back
Debut v Southport Central, FAC 1Q (a) 1.10.98, drawn 2-2
CAREER: Horwich. **Blackpool September 1898.**

A reserve half back whose two first team appearances came in FA Cup-ties. Having held Southport Central to a 2-2 draw in the away fixture, Blackpool were expected to progress in the replay at the Athletic Ground on 6th October, despite having lost the opening four Division Two matches. However, it was Southport who progressed, winning by 2-1 in a season when they finished as runners-up in the Lancashire League.
Appearances: FAC: 2 apps 0 gls Total: 2 apps 0 gls

HARRISON, William
Outside right
Debut v Glossop North End (a) 3.9.98, lost 1-4
CAREER: **Blackpool June 1898.** Earlestown January 1899, and re-signed September 1899.

Blackpool were a goal down after three minutes on the occasion of Harrison's debut, on the opening Saturday of the new season 1898-99. The kick off at Glossop was put back until 5.30 pm, to allow a cricket match, on the same field, to be finished. It was Glossop North End's first match in the Football League and they quite shook the football world by winning promotion to the First Division at the first time of asking. By contrast, Blackpool had to seek re-election, and then had to spend a season in the Lancashire League before returning to Division Two in 1900-01. Harrison commenced at outside right but was dropped after just two matches, and with only six League matches left to complete, the signing of J.J. Morris from Rock Ferry FC finally solved the problem position. Sadly, his four goals in six matches came just too late to lift the side clear of the last three places in the table and the unsuccessful application for re-election.
Appearances: FL: 3 apps 0 gls Total: 3 apps 0 gls

HATELY, Andrew Bone
Inside left 5' 10" 11st 7lbs
Born: Braithwaite, Cumberland, October quarter 1877
Died: Burnaby, British Columbia, 9th December 1955
Debut v Manchester City (h) 24.10.98, lost 2-4 (scored one goal)
CAREER: **Blackpool October 1898.** South Shore February 1899. Keswick FC August 1900. Penrith November 1905. Appleby September 1906, re-signed again up to & including September 1909.

Blackpool were quickly three goals down on the occasion of Andrew Hately's debut against Manchester City, one of City's goals scored by the famous Welsh international, Billy Meredith. After the interval Hately and Parkinson switched positions, and Blackpool, urged on by their supporters, roused themselves up, and from a neat pass from Leadbetter, Hately opened Blackpool's account. Hoyle scored a second, and a third all but followed from the same player within minutes, but Blackpool lost the stiring encounter 2-4. One week earlier they had been beaten 7-0 at Gainsborough Trinity, and two days after the defeat by Manchester City they lost 5-0 at Small Heath. They finished in 16th place in the table and were not re-elected. Hately, the son of a farmer, lived in Appleby, Westmorland, and was a plumber by occupation.
Appearances: FL: 1 app 1 gl Total: 1 app 1 gl

HAYWOOD, Adam
Inside forward 5' 5" 10st 6lbs
Born: Hominglow, near Burton-on-Trent, 23rd March 1874
Died: Dartford, Kent, April quarter 1932
Debut v Derby County (a) 30.11.07, lost 1-2
CAREER: Burton Ivanhoe. Swadlincote Town June 1895. Woolwich Arsenal January 1896. Burton Wanderers August 1898. New Whittingham Exchange September 1898. Glossop North End May 1899, fee £50. Queens Park Rangers August 1899. New Brompton 1900. Burton Swifts August 1900 Wolverhampton Wanderers June 1901. West Bromwich Albion May 1905. Cresswell United May 1907. **Blackpool November 1907**. Crystal Palace player-coach May 1908.

Adam Haywood made his Football League debut for Woolwich Arsenal against Leicester Fosse on 25th January 1896 and went on to record 84 League appearances and 31 goals, with an additional seven FA Cup appearances and five goals. By the time he reached Blackpool his career total amounted to 262 League matches and 84 goals, following lengthy spells with the Wolves (107 appearances and 28 goals) and West Bromwich Albion (62 appearances 25 goals). In his season at Bloomfield Road he made an excellent inside partner to the young amateur centre forward, W.A. Grundy, who enjoyed his best season in front of goal with 13 scored in 26 matches.
Appearances: FL: 15 apps 1 gl FAC: 1 app 0 gls Total: 16 apps 1 gl

HESLOP, Thomas 'Tom' W.

Inside forward
5' 11" 11st 2lbs
Born: Middlesbrough, 29th October 1897
Died: Bishop Auckland, 4th March 1958
Debut v Grimsby Town (a) 3.9.12, drawn 1-1 (scored)
CAREER: Middlesbrough August 1908. Birmingham July 1909. Shildon September 1910. Darlington April 1911. **Blackpool June 1912**. Bolton Wanderers November 1913. Leeds City November 1919. Accrington Stanley March 1920. Tranmere Rovers August 1921 to 1922.

Tom Heslop scored 14 goals for Darlington in season 1911-12, assisting his team to third place in the North Eastern League table. In the same season, Owers, a former Blackpool forward, was the Quakers'leading scorer with 19. During Blackpool's re-election season, Heslop was switched from inside forward to left half back, and his contribution was rewarded with a place on the retained list. Early in the following campaign, a move to Bolton Wanderers, of the First Division, brought little first team football, but he remained at Burnden Park until wartime season 1916-17, when he made 18 appearances and scored one goal. In post war football, eight appearances for Tranmere Rovers, of the Third Division North, wound up his career.
Appearances: FL: 29 apps 4 gls FAC: 2 apps 0 gls Total: 31 apps 4 gls

HEYWOOD, Frederick 'Fred'

Inside forward
5' 5" 10st 4lbs
Born: Edgworth, Lancashire, July quarter 1879
Died: Heywood, 2nd April 1962
Debut v Burslem Port Vale (a) 6.9.02, drawn 1-1 (scored)
CAREER: Turton. Newcastle United September 1900. **Blackpool June1902**. Reading cs 1903. **Blackpool again July 1904**. Oldham Athletic May 1905. Darwen August 1906. Turton November 1908. Chorley August 1909. Nelson November 1911. Hyde FC September 1912. Denton March 1914.

One of Blackpool's best early signings, Fred Heywood began with two and a half seasons with Turton. From there he had a big jump up to Newcastle United, with whom he spent two seasons. His style of play was described as "Scientific in character and quite delightful to watch. He is very speedy and often takes the ball in and amongst the opponents with ease, generally finishing up with a quick shot." Certainly, he vastly improved Blackpool's forward rank. His partnership with Harold Hardman made as good a left wing as ever played for the club. In 1911 he was employed as a publican at the Red Lion Inn at Tottington, near Bury.
Appearances: FL: 35 apps 4 gls FAC: 2 apps 0 gls Total: 37 apps 4 gls

HIGGINSON, William
Goalkeeper
Born: Wesham
Debut v Burton United (a) 14.9.01, drawn 1-1
CAREER: Kirkham. Garstang. **Blackpool August 1900 to 1902.** Lytham

Blackpool opened season 1901-02 with a goalkeeping crisis. In the season's opener, against Bristol City at Bloomfield Road, outfield player Harry Stirzaker appeared in goal in the 0-2 defeat. With reserve custodians Taylor and Dorrington unavailable an opportunity was given to Higginson, and he came out with flying colours. As one observer noted: "To accomplish such a performance, and under trying conditions, proves that he is possessed with any amount of skill and nerve. Higginson is a Wesham lad, and the only clubs that he has previously assisted are Kirkham and Garstang. When Blackpool do not require his services, he will play for Lytham."
Appearances: FL: 3 apps 0gls Total: 3 apps 0 gls

HOAD, Sidney 'Sid'James

Outside-right
5' 7½" 10st 5lbs
Born: Eltham, 27th December 1890
Died: Whitefield, 1st January 1973
Debut v Leeds City (a) 1.1.10, won 3-1
CAREER: St Annes. **Blackpool amateur December 1909**. Manchester City amateur May 1911. (RASC 31st March 1917.Wartime guest player with Tottenham Hotspur and Scotswood). Rochdale September 1920. Nelson January 1922. Hurst October 1927 to January 1929.

Sid Hoad began with Blackpool at 17 years of age and became their first international player when he was capped at amateur level by England in 1910-11, playing against Wales, Belgium and France. Training as a lawyer while playing his football as an amateur, he earned an upward move to First Division Manchester City, for whom he appeared in 69 League and Cup matches before the Great War. He subsequently enlisted in the Army in March 1917 as a motor mechanic, and served in France as a driver. He was discharged with nervous exhaustion but happily made a full recovery. In September 1920 he joined Rochdale, at that time operating in the Central League. In the following term he made his debut in the newly formed Division Three North, moving in mid season to join Nelson, where he won a championship medal in season 1922-23. In later years he was, quite unusually, an abstemious and non-smoking licensee in Lancaster. His overall career figures for his four League clubs totalled 272 League and Cup matches and 20 goals.
Appearances: FL: 26 apps 3 gls FAC: 3 apps 0 gls Total: 29 apps 3 gls
Honours: England Amateur International, 3 caps 1910-11. (Nelson) FL Division Three North champions 1923.

HODGSON, James
Goalkeeper
Debut v Grimsby Town (h) 27.2.04, won 3-0
CAREER: Poulton. **Blackpool January 1903.**

The Blackpool pitch was almost unfit for play on the occasion of the debut of James Hodgson, who kept goal in Arthur Hull's absence, but a covering of snow and slush did not prevent the home team from playing some outstanding football in the wretched conditions. Grimsby Town, who were last season in the First Division, were overplayed. They conceded two penalties and, in the second half, their defender George McDiarmid, having twice been cautioned, was sent off the field for commiting a bad foul on 'Geordie' Anderson. Hodgson in goal opened rather shakily, but soon improved, and gave evidence that he would be a valuable man in an emergency, without being expected to mount a serious challenge to Arthur Hull for the first team jersey.
Appearances: FL: 2 apps 0 gls Total: 2 apps 0 gls

HOGG, Robert 'Bobby'
Inside forward 5' 8" 12st 7lbs
Born: Whitburn, County Durham, 20th March 1877
Died: Malton, Yorkshire, 4th March 1963
Debut v Leicester Fosse (h) 3.9.04, drawn 0-0
CAREER: Selbourne Rovers. Whitburn FC. South Shields June 1898. Sunderland June 1899. Grimsby Town November 1902. **Blackpool August 1904**. Luton Town May 1905.

Bobby Hogg gained an inter-league medal early in his professional career while enjoying a fair slice of first team action with Sunderland. Without a doubt his best season at Roker was the 1901-02 Championship triumph when he made 29 appearances and scored six goals. A recurring knee injury blighted his spell with Grimsby Town, but he recovered sufficiently to play in 30 matches for Blackpool. In Second Division matches only 36 goals were scored in 38 matches; Blackpool, however, enjoyed a good run in the Cup coming through qualifying rounds three, four, five and six before being narrowly beaten by 2-1 at Bristol City.
Appearances: FL: 26 apps 5 gls FAC: 4 apps 1 gl Total: 30 apps 6 gls
Honours: FL representative v Irish League 1901. (Sunderland) FL Division One champions 1902.

HOLLINGWORTH, John D.
Outside left
Debut v Bristol City (h) 27.1.06, lost 1-3
CAREER: Rossall. Tonge F.C. **Blackpool amateur January 1906.**

In a season when Blackpool struggled in Division Two but reached the third round of the FA Cup for the first time, the November transfer of Charles Bennett to Bradford City effectively robbed the team of its best forward. In addition, the outside left position was not successfully filled following the departure of both Marshall McEwan, to Everton, and John Waddington, to Southport Central, in 1904-05. John Hollingworth was a mid term recruit who was described as playing the typical amateur game. Slim, and quick off the mark, he enjoyed a fair amount of senior action before losing out to local amateur wingman Robert Topping in the final two months of the seaon.
Appearances: FL: 10 apps 0 gls FAC: 1 app 0 gls Total: 11 apps 0 gls

HOWARD, John H.
Outside right
Debut v Huddersfield Town (a) 27.4.12, lost 0-4
CAREER: Burton All Saints September 1911. **Blackpool April 1912.** Burton All Saints May 1912.

Despite being considered "The best of the five forwards" in one press report, John Howard's debut at Leeds Road resulted in a heavy 4-0 defeat. Blackpool fielded an unfamiliar eleven for the last match of the season, Howard and Metcalf formed the right wing and Spencer appeared with Dale at full back. It was an unbalanced team, and the Huddersfield Town eleven proved altogether too good for Blackpool in the finer points of the game. Howard and Metcalf were sometimes troublesome to the Town defence, and Fiske kept goal well, but Huddersfield finished off their season in fine style, their 4-0 victory being well deserved.
Appearances: FL: 1 app 0 gls Total: 1 app 0 gls

HOWSON, Edward Bamber
Right half back 5' 9"
Born: Blackpool, 25th March 1876
Died: Blackpool, 17th May 1947
Debut v Small Heath (a) 26.12.98, lost 0-5
CAREER: Haydock FC. Earlestown FC. Lytham FC 1897. **Blackpool October 1898.**

Edward Howson assisted Haydock FC to two Lancashire Alliance championships before joining Lytham from Earlestown for a season from 1897. An initial outing, at inside right, on Boxing Day, resulted in a heavy defeat at Small Heath, and the remainder of his first team appearances were made as a wing half back, but with little success as Blackpool experienced their first relegation after just three seasons in Division Two. Initially employed as a blacksmith's apprentice, Howson served in the RGA during the First World War. In 1939 he was working as a blacksmith by the Public Water Supply Authority, and was later a garage proprietor. Brother of Richard (q.v.)
Appearances: FL: 8 apps 0 gls Total: 8 apps 0 gls

HOWSON, Richard
Half back
Born: Blackpool October quarter 1877 (Baptised 28th October 1877)
Died: Blackpool, 30th March 1929
Debut v Glossop (a) 3.9.98, lost 1-4
CAREER: Fleetwood Rangers October 1897. **Blackpool May 1898**. Blackpool Etrurians April 1901.

A September 1896 match report of a Fleetwood Rangers match against Prescott considered that: "Howson, the new centre forward of Fleetwood Rangers, started very well, and showed that he knows how to shoot. He is speedy, has any amount of dash, but often kicks too high and hard when passing, yet should make a capital centre forward when he becomes a little more polished. He is, as it where, a diamond in the rough." Some two years later he joined Blackpool, whose selectors fielded him in all half back positions and three different positions in the front line. When Blackpool resumed in Division Two, after a season out in1899-1900, Howson appeared in only three League matches and was released in the close season. In 1911 he was employed as a gas meter inspector.
Appearances: FL: 18 apps 0 gls FAC: 2 apps 0 gls Total: 20 apps 0 gls

HOYLE, Thomas
Right half back
Debut v New Brighton Tower (a) 5.11.98, lost 0-4
CAREER: Fleetwood Rangers. **Blackpool October 1898.**

One week after assisting Fleetwood Rangers to beat Rochdale 1-0 in the Second Qualifying Round of the Lancashire Cup, Thomas Hoyle was signed by Blackpool. He was ineligible to assist his new team in the competition, and on 5th December, Blackpool lost 1-0 to Bolton Wanderers who went on to reach the Final, won 3-1 by Bury. In terms of League action, Hoyle's chief asset was his wonderful faculty of filling all sorts of positions, his 19 appearances being made in both wing half berths, and in three different forward positions
Appearances: FL: 19 apps 1 gl Total: 19 apps 1 gl

HUGHES, David
Left half back
Debut v Gainsborough Trinity (a) 21.11.03, lost 1-3
CAREER: Aberdare. **Blackpool May 1903**

One of five players to make a single appearance in 1903-04, David Hughes deputised for Edward Threlfall at Gainsborough Trinity in a disappointing display. Considering the fact that Blackpool had the full benefit of a gale of wind in the first half, they failed to do themselves justice, and were two goals down at the interval. Three goals in arrears shortly after the restart, Blackpool's late reply was a rare goal from Billy Anderton, normally seen on the right wing, but fielded at inside right. The Blackpool attack featured two newcomers, Peter Miller on the right wing and Lewis Swarbrick on the left.
Appearances: FL: 1 app 0 gls Total: 1 app 0 gls

HULL, Arthur Alexander 'Tishy'

Goalkeeper
Born: Birkenhead, 16th March 1878
Died: 1952 (Buried at Barton upon Irwell on 23rd August.)
Debut v Barnsley (a) 10.1.03, lost 0-6
CAREER: Blackpool September 1902 to May 1906. Pendlebury June 1907. Mirfield United October 1907. Grimsby Town August 1908. Wirral Railway September 1909. Wath Athletic April 1910. Tyldesley Albion September 1910.

Considering the fact that Arthur Hull had not kept goal until joining Blackpool – he had previously play rugby in Cheshire – the very tall and mustachiode custodian ensured that Blackpool's tradition for good goalkeepers was in safe hands. Good alike with high and low shots, he maintained a very high level of skill and cool judgment throughout. As one observer noted in February 1906: "Hull the Blackpool goalkeeper is playing very well this season, and against Glossop last week he was steady throughout. In six games this season he has been unbeaten, and on nine occasions has conceded only one goal." The 1939 Census revealed that Arthur Hull was working as a civil service clerk for The Ministry of Labour while living in Eccles.
Appearances: FL: 116 apps 0 gls FAC: 11 apps 0 gls Total: 127 apps 0 gls

JOHNSON, Samuel 'Sam' Clay
Half back 5' 10"
Born: Manchester, 7th June 1881
Died: Birch Hill Hospital, Wardle, Lancashire, 21st November1962
Debut v Gainsborough Trinity (h) 16.9.05, drawn 2-2
CAREER: Newton Heath Athletic 1896. Nelson. Tonge 1899. Newton Heath January 1901. Heywood United November 1902. Colne January 1904. **Blackpool May 1905.** Brynn Central February 1907. Colne September 1907. Exeter City May 1908. Coventry City June 1909. Leeds City June 1911. Colne September 1912. Eccles Borough later in the same month. Macclesfield December 1913. Vickers Sports December 1912.

Sam Johnson's best season in League football was his first at Bloomfield Road in which he appeared in 25 League and five FA Cup-ties, winning the left half back spot from Luke Raisbeck in November and missing just one League match thereafter. In the following season he lost his first team place to Tom Clarke and departed to Brynn Central later in the campaign. The best of his subsequent work came in Lancashire Combination circles. In his second of three separate spells with Colne AFC his reputation soared when he scored 27 goals from centre half back, his total including one four goal haul and two hat tricks. On leaving Colne for the last time, he assisted Eccles Borough to the championship of the First Division of the Lancashire Combination. Outside of the game he worked as a boot repairer, and in the years leading up to World War Two he was living in Fleetwood and working as a Football Pools Agent. His wife, Julia, was a greengrocer.
Appearances: FL: 33 apps 1 gl FAC: 5 apps 0 gls Total: 38 apps 1 gl

JOLLY, Alfred
Outside right 5' 10" 12st 9lbs
Born: Ribby with Wrea, 17th April 1879
Died: Blackpool, 29th March 1969
Debut v West Bromwich Albion (a) 7.11.04, lost 2-4
CAREER: Glentoran. **Blackpool November 1904.** Southport Central cs to November 1905. Atherton Church House January 1906. Brynn Central December 1906.

In August 1904 the 'Manchester Evening News' included Alfred Jolly in a list of Blackpool signings. The fact that the Blackpool club did not immediately register him with the Football League suggested that he was not expected to be involved above reserve team level. However, his first opportunity came when John Scott was injured at Liverpool on 5th November and was not recovered in time to travel to West Bromwich Albion just two days later. With a reserve goalkeeper, Dorrington, and an out-of-position left back in Jolly, Blackpool's unfamiliar line-up went under by four goals to two. Some four months later, a second opportunity arose when Marshall McEwan was transferred to Everton. John Waddington switched across from right wing to left, and Jolly was given a four match run at outside right that included wins against Burton United and Burslem Port Vale. However, Jolly and Waddington were released in the close season, and both joined Southport Central.
Appearances: FL: 5 apps 0 gls Total: 5 apps 0 gls

JONES, Frank
Inside right
Debut v Burnley (a) 13.4.1901, lost 0-4
CAREER: South Shore June 1899. **Blackpool April 1901.**

Frank Jones' debut at Turf Moor coincided with a benefit for Joe Taylor, Burnley's captain. The home side were dominant throughout, McLintock netting four goals, two from the penalty spot. On the award of the second penalty, after 75 minutes, Blackpool's goalkeeper Dorrington was sent off for too strongly disputing the award. Stirzaker took over in goal, and his first involvement was picking the ball out of the net as McLinlock registered his fourth goal. Blackpool's forwards were largely ineffective throughout, although Frank Jones came near to scoring with a looping header in the second half which was acrobatically tipped over the crossbar by Burnley goalkeeper Collins.
Appearances: FL 1 app 0 gls Total: 1 app 0 gls

JONES, James 'Jimmy'

Full-back
5' 7½" 10st 9lbs
Born: South Bank, 9 July 1888
Died: Blackpool, October quarter 1952
Debut v Fulham (h) 28.9.12, won 2-0
CAREER: Gateshead Co-op. Gateshead F.C. August 1911. **Blackpool June 1912.** Bolton Wanderers March 1920, fee £1,000. New Brighton August 1922, retired cs 1927.

Jimmy Jones was hardly the build of most full backs of his day, but his chief assets were steady judgment and coolness under pressure. In 1913 the 'Lancashire Post Annual' considered him; "Perhaps the best player at Bloomfield Road. He filled the eye all last season, and will go far in football." His period with Blackpool spanned the Great War and in August 1917 the 'Liverpool Echo' reported as follows: "Private James Jones, of the Machine Gun Corps, and former full back and skipper of the Blackpool team, has written from France to contradict rumours that he had been killed. He says: "I am still alive, and kicking a ball about whenever I get a chance." Transferred to Bolton Wanderers in March 1920, his best season at Burnden Park was 1920-21, when he made 33 First Division appearances in the side that chased the title but finished third behind Burnley and Manchester City. He had made 70 League appearances for Bolton before losing his place to Alec Finney, the former New Brighton full-back who won an FA Cup medal in his first season and went on to complete 530 League and Cup appearances for the Trotters. Jones joined New Brighton in the season prior to Football League entry and captained the team when they commenced in the Third Division North in season 1923-24, remarkably consistent, he missed very few matches despite being well into the veteran stage, finally retiring at the age of 39. He scored just one goal in his overall 324 League appearances, this being the winner for New Brighton in a 1-0 victory against Hartlepools United at Rake Lane in November 1923. His wind-assisted clearance from the halfway line completely deceiving Summerfield, the Hartlepools goalkeeper.
Appearances: FL: 112 apps 0 gls FAC: 3 apps 0 gls Total: 115 apps 0 gls

JONES, John
Inside left
Debut v Glossop (a) 3.9.98, lost 1-4
CAREER: Fleetwood Rangers September 1897. **Blackpool May to October 1898.**

A season with Fleetwood Rangers preceded John Jones' transfer to Blackpool, but his stay at the Athletic Ground was fleeting. His four League outings were made consecutively from the start of 1898-99, and each ended in defeat. It was the season in which Blackpool lost their Division Two status, but Jones had departed long before the axe fell, having been released in mid October.
Appearances: FL: 4 apps 0 gls Total: 4 apps 0 gls

JONES, John (No 2)

Left half back
Debut v Lincoln City (a) 19.9.03, drawn 0-0
CAREER: Blackburn Rovers September 1902. **Blackpool September 1903 to 1906.**

The bulk of John Jones' appearances came in his first season when he was described as: "A quick and forceful tackler, better in defence than attack." He also proved to be, in an emergency, a more than capable goalkeeper. This situation occurred on 20th February when Arthur Hull was unavailable, and with no deputy on hand, captain Bob Birket recommended Jones for the position, and sportingly, Jones agreed to tackle it. After he had conceded the first goal Jones improved considerably, the Lancashire Evening Post' considering that: "Some of his saves were worthy of McBride." (McBride being the celebrated Preston North End and Scotland goalkeeper.)
Appearances: FL: 17 apps 0 gls FAC: 2 apps 0 gls Total: 19 apps 0 gls

KEARNS, Alfred 'Alfie'
Inside right
Born: Falls Road, Belfast, 7th February 1877
Debut v Leicester Fosse (h) 3.9.04, drawn 0-0
CAREER: Belfast Celtic. Belfast Distillery. **Blackpool May 1904**. St Helens Recreation May 1905. St Helens Town March 1906. Belfast Distillery.

There was no getting away from the fact that the Blackpool team of season 1904-05 did not play up to expectations. The forward line in particular was an acute disappointment, containing as it did an England international (Chadwick), an Irish international (Kearns) and an inter-league player (Morgan), a Scottish junior international (McEwan) and a centre forward with plenty of experience in the First Division, including a championship medal with Sunderland (Hogg). Alfie Kearns had been awarded international and inter-league honours in Ireland, but he lost his place at Blackpool after appearing in the first nine matches of the season and made infrequent appearances thereafter. A season in Division Two of the Lancashire Combination with St Helens Town was followed by a return to Ireland, but he did not figure in Distillery's Irish Cup Final victory against Shelbourne in 1905.
Appearances: FL: 15 apps 3 gls FAC: 3 apps 0 gls Total: 18 apps 3 gls
Honours: N. Ireland International, 6 caps, 1900-02. Irish League representative, 3 apps. 1900-01. (Distillery) Irish Cup winner 1903.

KEECH, William 'Bill'

Utility
5' 9" 12st 0lbs
Born: Irthlingborough, Northants, 22nd February 1872
Died: Paddington, 6th September 1948
Debut v Burnley (a) 4.9.97, lost 1-5
CAREER: Irthlingborough Revellers 1888. Irthlingborough FC 1889. Wellingborough 1890. Finedon September 1891. Northamptonshire County Xl (versus Norfolk County) January 1892. Kettering Hawks. Irthlingborough Wanderers. Kettering August 1894, Barnsley St Peters September 1894. Liverpool September 1895.. Barnsley cs1896. **Blackpool July 1897**. Leicester Fosse April 1898. Loughborough February 1899. Queens Park Rangers August 1899. Woolwich Arsenal May 1901. Brentford May 1902. Small Heath December 1903. Irthingborough FC September 1904. Kendal Rise United July 1904. Birkenhead August 1905. Queens Park Rangers trainer. Brentford trainer 1914-15.

An all round sportsman with honours in skating and boxing, Bill Keech could also play in any position in the half back line. Although no explanation was forthcoming, in February 1898 he was suspended 'sine die' by the Blackpool club, the 'Lancashire Evening Post' commenting: "This is a pity, as he was a stopgap where ever one was needed." Some later evidence of his versatility came with Loughborough, who used him exclusively as a centre forward, scoring six goals in 13 Division Two matches. He was later a member of Queens Park Rangers' first professional side, and his younger brother, Ben, also played for the Rangers. On retirement from the game he worked as a landlord in various public houses in the London area, one of which, 'The Royal Standard' in Euston was destroyed by incendiary fire in September 1940. On retirement from the licensed trade he was a billiards marker at the 'Elephant and Castle' on Harrow Road.
Appearances: FL: 16 apps 0 gls FAC: 1 app 0 gls Total: 17 apps 0 gls.

KEENAN, Harold

Centre half back
5' 8" 11st 7lbs
Born: Warrington, 20th December 1893
Died: Winwick, Lancashire, 29th August 1956
Debut v Fulham (a) 15.1.13, lost 2-4
CAREER: Atherton. **Blackpool December 1912 to 1923.**

A very lengthy spell with Blackpool commenced as a teenager, and in three seasons before League football was suspended due to the Great War, Harold Keenan had just two first team appearances to his name. After serving in the Prince of Wales Volunteers (4th Battalion Lancashire Regiment) during the period of hostilities, he returned as a key figure in Blackpool's middle line, the team reaching fourth position in Division Two in each of seasons 1919-20 (In which he was awarded a benefit of £300) and 1920-21. Elected captain, by the other players, when George Wilson left for Sheffield Wednesday in March 1920, Keenan combined skill with determination and had a big share in Blackpool's excellent start to life after the rigours of war. Sadly, his final two seasons were blighted by rheumatic gout, which kept him sidelined for lengthy periods.
Appearances: FL: 102 apps 3 gls FAC: 7 apps 0 gls Total: 109 apps 3 gls

KIDD, James 'Jimmy'

Goalkeeper
5' 11" 12st 7lbs
Born: Darlington, 3rd June 1881
Died: Blackpool, April quarter 1955
Debut v West Bromwich Albion (h) 8.4.11, drawn 0-0
CAREER: Spennymoor United November 1908. **Blackpool July 1910.** Bolton Wanderers March 1915. Derby County September 1919. Fleetwood August 1923.

Brilliant displays by Jimmy Kidd for Spennymoor United assisted his team to the championship of the North Eastern League in season 1909-10. Joining Blackpool, as understudy to consistent goalkeeper Bill Fiske - with over 200 League appearances - Kidd's opportunities in the League side were limited. His opportunity came, however, when Fiske was transferred to Nottingham Forest in May 1914, and an unbroken run of 31 matches was rewarded when Bolton Wanderers, of the First Division, stepped in for his services. The FA Cup semi-finalists had been looking for some time to strengthen their defence, having tried a succession of goalkeepers without much success. A goalless encounter at Notts County on his debut was an excellent start, and was quickly followed by similar scorelines at Newcastle United and Middlesbrough. Sadly, having appeared in earlier rounds of the FA Cup with Blackpool, Kidd was ineligable to assist Bolton in their Cup run, which ended, after extra time, by a 1-2 defeat against Sheffield United at Ewood Park, Blackburn. When League football was suspended for the duration, Kidd's sojourn at Burnden Park came to a close. After the war he joined Derby County, and was cast in a familiar role of reserve goalkeeper, appearing in 21 League and Cup matches in three seasons. In 1939 he was working as a tram driver and living at 39 Shetland Road, Blackpool.
Appearances: FL: 65 apps 0 gls FAC: 5 apps 0 gls Total: 70 apps 0 gls

KILLEAN, Edward 'Ted'

Utility
5' 9" 11st 6lbs
Born: Great Harwood, July quarter 1874
Died: Fylde, October quarter 1937, age 63
Debut v Bradford City (h) 26.12.03, lost 0-1
CAREER: Army football (North Lancashire Regiment and 3rd Coldstream Guards). Blackburn Rovers August 1894. Glossop North End November 1898, fee £70. Southampton November 1900. New Brompton (loan) October 1901. Southampton November 1901. **Blackpool December 1903.**

Ted Killean made 97 first team appearances for Blackburn Rovers. As a player of dual capacity, he began in the forward line but settled at wing half, where his constructive work and prompting were best utilised. Glossop also took full advantage of his versatility, fielding him in no fewer than six different outfield positions in his second season at North Road. A move south proved unrewarding, as he was unable to break into a strong Southampton side and spent a brief loan spell with New Brompton. He returned to his native Lancashire in December 1903 to join Blackpool, but appeared in only three League matches. A Boxing Day defeat, when he deputised at left full back for Bob Birket, was followed by a draw at Barnsley and a home win against Lincoln City, when he appeared at left half back in place of the injured Tom Wolstenholme. In earlier days, he appeared in the Blackburn County Police Court in May 1899 for a breach of the peace – fighting in Whalley Road. He was bound over for £5.
Appearances: FL: 3 apps 0 gls Total: 3 apps 0 gls

-KING, Horace Herbert

Inside left
5' 6" 10st 9lbs
Born: Norwich, 10th July 1883
Died: Norwich, 4th February1940
Debut v Stockport County (a) 2.9.07, drawn 1-1
CAREER: Angel Road School. Norwich St James. Catton November 1900. Norwich City September 1903. Norfolk County 1903-06. **Blackpool May 1907.**

One of a trio of former Norwich City players who joined Blackpool in the summer of 1907, Horace King and Bill Fiske being followed in less than a month by Horace Brindley. Of the three, Bill Fiske was the most successful, while Horace King, a short but sturdy inside forward, was desperately unfortunate to sustain a career ending broken leg injury on his tenth appearance. It was shortly after the interval in the match against West Bromwich Albion at Bloomfield Road that King and Young, the Albion full back, kicked a ball simultaneously, resulting in King's left leg being broken. In a rather graphic account in the local press it was stated that the snap was distinctly heard by most of those present, and several lady spectators fainted. To add insult to injury, it took several minutes before a stretcher could be found to take the unfortunate player to hospital. A collection for him was taken at full time.
Appearances: FL: 10 apps 1 gl Total: 10 apps 1 gl

KING, Thomas Frederick
Centre forward
Debut v Lincoln City (a) 11.3.99, drawn 0-0
CAREER: Blackpool Grammar School. **Blackpool amateur March 1898, re-signed June 1900.**

Blackpool were without centre forward Bob Birket, who had suffered a family bereavement, for the trip to Lincoln and hurried arrangements were made to register Thomas King, a young player from Blackpool Grammar School. It was noted at the time that Frank Williams (q.v.) an assistant schoolmaster who also signed from the local Grammar School, had proved to be an outstanding success, and it was hoped that King would be equally successful. Sadly, this did not come about although King was re-signed when Blackpool resumed in Division Two, following their relegation in 1899-1900.
Appearances: FL: 1 app 0 gls Total: 1 app 0 gls

KIRBY, Conyers
Outside right 5' 7" 11st 0lbs
Born: Bordesley Green 18th March 1884
Died: Isleworth, London, 9th April 1946
Debut v Leeds City (h) 14.9.07, lost 2-3
CAREER: Army Medical Corps. Fulham April 1905. Birmingham May 1906. **Blackpool June 1907.** Worcester City December 1907. Kidderminster Harriers. Willenhall Pickwick. Fulham 1913. CE Europa manager 1922. FC Barcelona manager 1924. Athletico Bilbao manager September 1925 to1926.

Conyers Kirby first worked as a railway clerk and during the World War One period enlisted in the RAMC, rising to the rank of

Staff Sergeant. In terms of a football career, he played in the League just once for Birmingham and twice for Blackpool, but subsequently embarked on a continental managerial career, combining this with refereeing duties in Spain, returning to England in 1926. Apparently, despite his unusual forename, he was known to his family as "Ralph".
Appearances: FL: 2 apps 0 gls Total: 2 apps 0 gls

LANE, James 'Joe' Charles

Forward
5' 9" 11st 5lbs
Born: Hertford, Watford, 1st June 1892
Died: Abbots Langley, Hertfordshire, 27th February 1959
Debut v Leeds City (h) 22.11.13, drawn 2-2 (scored one goal)
CAREER: Watford Wednesday. Watford FC amateur 1909. Ferencvaros Torna (Budapest). 1910. Watford 1911. Sunderland July 1913. **Blackpool November 1913, fee £400.** (Served during WW1 with the Hertford Yeomanry in Egypt). Birmingham March 1920, fee £3,300 (A record, of which the player was said to have received one third). Millwall Athletic August 1922. Barcelona coach August 1924. Sittingbourne April 1925. Ellesmere Port Town (trial) August 1925. Eccles United August 1926. Bournville November 1929. Watford Printing Works FC circa 1936.

Follow a brief four months with Sunderland and a much longer war-interrupted time with Blackpool, Joe Lane became a well-known figure in the immediate post-war seasons. Joe's forte was his sharpshooting, a quality evident throughout his career. At times inclined to be too individualistic he nevertheless continued his success with Blackpool by assisting Birmingham to promotion in their 1921 championship team. A printer by calling, he came from a well-to-do family – his father owned a printing company, and his 1910-11 Hungarian exile came about by a printing assignment in that country. Joe served in Eygypt during World War One with the Hertfordshire Yeomandry. He was still turning out with the Watford Printing Works team beyond his 40th year.
Appearances: FL: 93 apps 66 gls FAC: 5 apps 0 gls Total: 98 apps 66 gls
Honours: (Birmingham) FL Division 2 champions 1921.

LATHERON, Robert
Outside left 5' 6½" 11st 4lbs
Born: Carlin How, Redcar, 3rd July 1879
Died: Luton, July quarter 1957
Debut v Tottenham Hotspur (h) 10.10.08, drawn 1-1
CAREER: Luton Town September 1905, and re-signed May 1906 and April 1907. **Blackpool May 1908, released with a free transfer September 1911.**

Robert Latheron's debut, and single senior appearance, came against Tottenham Hotspur, making their first visit to Blackpool, having previously been members of Southern League. Neither team were fully represented, Spurs missing their famous centre, Vivian Woodward, who was engaged in an Inter-League match in Belfast. Blackpool were missing four regular first teamers through injury or illness, and under the circumstances played a far better game than was anticipated, and thoroughly deserved a share of the points, their dash and vim more than compensating for their lack of polish. On his debut Latheron rattled the crossbar with a snap shot in the first half, and later spent some time off the field having hurt his shoulder in a fall. The local correspondent noted that Blackpool had maintained their unbeaten home record, but the forward line lost many opportunities due to lack of understanding. Latheron enlisted in the 5th Battalion Bedfordshire Regiment on 10th November 1914. He transferred to the London Regiment and then the Royal Engineers from 6th June 1917. He served in France from 29th August to 21st October 1919, apart from a period in rehabilitation following a gunshot wound in October 1916. He survived the war, but sadly three of his brothers did not – Walter died in May 1915; Edwin in October 1917 and William in June 1918. Younger

brother, Edwin Latheron, was an England international who appeared in 257 League matches for Blackburn Rovers.
Appearances: FL: 1 app 0 gls Total: 1 app 0 gls

LAVERY, James Leonard

Forward
Born: Liverpool, 28th August 1880
Died: 1961
Debut v Clapton Orient (a) 23.12.05, drawn 0-0
CAREER: Dumfries F.C. **Blackpool July 1905 to 1907.**

James Lavery, who had assisted Dumfries FC to reach the final of the Dumfries & Galloway Cup, appeared in the original fixture, which ended in a draw, against Douglas Wanderers, but had left to join Blackpool before the replay was contested. He was doubtless pleased that his former colleagues won the replay 2-1, but sorry that he had missed the opportunity to win a medal. In his first season with Blackpool he had some time to wait for a first team opportunity, but was part of a successful Reserve team who won promotion from Division Two of the Lancashire Combination as runners-up to Colne AFC. An accident in his place of work caused him to miss a large part of his second season. **Note**: A player named J. Lavery played for the following clubs: South Shields Adelaide (July 1910), Hebburn Argyle (August 1900), Seaham Villa (September 1911), Tunstall Park (November 1911) and Hebburn Argyle again (August 1912.) It has not been possible, however, to confirm that this is the same player as the above.
Appearances: FL: 23 apps 2 gls Total: 23 apps 2 gls

LEADBETTER, John 'Jack'
Outside left 5' 6" 10st 10lbs
Born: Fleetwood, 4th June 1873
Died: Fleetwood, 21st November 1956
Debut v Burnley (h) 11.9.97, drawn 1-1
CAREER: Fleetwood Rangers 1893. Chorley April 1895. **Blackpool August 1897 and re-signed November 1900**. Fleetwood Amateurs. Royston Red Rose July 1902.

Born at Fleetwood and a trawler fisherman by trade, Jack Leadbetter was a diminutive winger who was able to find his way through through the most compact defences on his day. In Blackpool's relegation season one observer commented: "Leadbetter is decidedly the best forward in the Blackpool team, and is to be complimented on the gallant efforts he is making to pull the front rank together." Sadly, his efforts were not sufficient to lift his team out of the re-election places, depite his scoring in victories against Darwen and Gainsborough Trinity in the final month of the campaign.
Appearances: FL: 63 apps 10 gls FAC: 3 apps 3 gls Total: 66 apps 13 gls

LOWE, Wallace E. P.

Right full back
5' 10" 10st 12lbs
Born: Blackpool, 17th April 1884
Died: Blackpool, July quarter 1942
Debut v Barnsley (a) 10.9.04, lost 1-2
CAREER: Blackpool Park Road. Blackpool Standard. Poulton. Ashton Wanderers December 1902. **Blackpool amateur May 1904.** Blackpool Athletic. **Blackpool August 1908**. Blackpool Athletic November 1908. Colne January 1909. Bacup August 1909. Lytham Athletic October 1911.

Despite being lightly built for a full-back, Wallace Lowe reached League level with Blackpool. His several junior clubs included a start with Blackpool Park Road, later with Blackpool Standard and Poulton. He made his Football League debut for Blackpool at Barnsley on 10th September 1904 in a 1-2 defeat. Mainly in reserve throughout, his best seasonal return was five consecutive matches in 1905-06. His final appearance, three years on from his debut, came at Gainsborough Trinity, in a 1-2 defeat on 28th September 1907. He was operating with Blackpool Athletic when Colne signed him in November 1908. Despite a winning debut against Bury Reserve, Lowe faced stiff competition from

several defenders, including Sam Speakman, brother of the Liverpool outside-right. A late rally saved Colne from relegation in a trying season when every member of the side had been absent at some time or other, throughout the campaign. In the summer Wallace Lowe left to join Bacup, members of Division Two of the Lancashire Combination. In 1901 his father, Peter, was employed as a barge boatman, with his son Wallace working as a plasterer.
Appearances: FL: 11 apps 0 gls Total: 11 apps 0 gls

LYON, Herbert Henry Saxon Bertie Cordey 'Bertie'

Inside forward
5' 7" 11st 8lbs
Born: Mosbrough, Yorkshire, 18th May 1875
Died: Tredegar, Monmouthshire, 29th April 1927
Debut v Barnsley (h) 2.9.08, drawn 1-1
CAREER: Overseal Town September 1895. Gresley Rovers May 1896. Leicester Fosse January 1899, fee £50 Nelson June 1900. Watford June 1901. Reading May 1902. West Ham United May 1903. Brighton & Hove Albion May 1904. Swindon Town May 1905. Carlisle United May 1906. Swindon Town again May 1907. **Blackpool June 1908**, fee £35. Walsall July 1909. Tredegar August 1910.

Bertie Lyon began in League football with Leicester Fosse, his 15 appearances and five goals including an appearance as goalkeeper, against Bolton Wanderers in March 1900, in which he remained undefeated. He had assisted a further eight clubs before joining Blackpool for a season spent mainly in reserve. It is worth noting that at birth he was named just 'Herbert'. On his marriage to Edith Shaw in October 1899 he was registered as Herbert Henry Saxon Lyon. His death was recorded as Herbert Henry Lyon. His son (1906-1999) was named Herbert Harry Saxon Lyon, but he was unable to shed any light onto the confusion. Among Bertie's many employments were spells as a hotel waiter, a butcher, a collier and a brickyard labourer.
Appearances: FL: 8 apps 2 gls FAC: 1 app 0 gls Total: 9 apps 2 gls
Honours: (Carlisle United) Lancashire Combination Division Two champions 1907.

McCULLOCH, James

Centre half back 5' 11½" 12st 3lbs
Born: Blantyre
Debut v Glossop (h) 18.1.13, drawn 1-1
CAREER: Everton. **Blackpool January 1913.**

Signed from Everton as cover at centre half back for James Connor, McCulloch was unlikely to claim a permanent place in the centre of defence, with his fellow Scot well established. Nevertheless, McCulloch had an early opportunity against Glossop, with Connor sidelined and three other regular members of the first team – Wilson, Booth and Quinn – all out injured following a bruising FA Cup-tie at Tottenham Hotspur just two days earlier. Sadly, McCulloch, who was just getting into his stride, quickly joined the list of casualties with a serious head injury, when an opponent's elbow struck him in the face. The unfortunate ex-Evertonian dropped to the floor, and after receiving some attention on the pitch, was carried off, and did not return.
Appearances: FL: 1 app 0 gls Total: 1 app 0 gls

McEWAN, Marshall

Outside left
Born: Rutherglen, 10th April 1884
Died: Belfast, 6th January 1966
Debut v Bristol City (a) 5.12.03, lost 0-5
CAREER: Glencairn Juniors 1901. Everton December 1902. **Blackpool December 1903**. Bolton Wanderers April 1905, fee £300. Chelsea March 1910, fee £1,000. Linfield 1911. Fleetwood.

A worthy successor to earlier wing forwards Jack Cox and Harold Hardman, Marshall McEwan joined Blackpool at 19 years of age,

having first played as a junior with Glencairn. He was signed by Everton in December 1902, but was transferred to Blackpool without having made a first team appearance. In April 1904, the 'Lancashire Evening Post' had this to say: "Playing at outside left McEwan delighted spectators by his spirited dashes. Very speedy on the track, he kept up his pace in possession of the ball, and the brilliant goal that he scored against Woolwich Arsenal, when he ran half the length of the field, will long be remembered. He gets off the mark smartly, and either shoots or centres excellently. In Bennett he has a good partner." An early press report, following his transfer to Bolton Wanderers, considered: "McEwan, the former Blackpool player, has turned out to be a splendid signing by the Wanderers. He is fleet of foot, can dribble, and rarely fails to drop the ball in front of goal. The pity was that these extraordinary bits of accurate work went for nothing." In four seasons at Burden Park McEwan appeared in 152 League matches and scored 15 goals. Chelsea was his final League club, but his signing came too late in the season to save his new club from relegation from Division One. Placed on Chelsea's transfer list with a fee of £1,000 on his head, McEwan joined Linfield. Many years later he was voted the eighth best Linfield player of all time. Sadly he had no close relatives at his death and was buried by the Belfast Welfare Authority at the City Cemetery.
Appearances: FL: 44 apps 1 gl FAC: 6 apps 2 gls Total: 50 apps 3 gls
Honours: Scottish Junior international. Irish League representative, 10 apps. 1911-19. (Linfield) Irish Cup Winners 1913, 1915, 1916 and 1919.

McHARDY, David Durward
Centre half back
Born: Monifieth, County of Forfar, 10th September 1869
Died: Auchtermuchly, Fife, 14th September 1903
Debut v Burnley (a) 4.9.97, lost 1-5
CAREER: Glossop North End. **Blackpool June 1897**. Warmley FC. June 1898.

David McHardy crossed the border to join Glossop North End, and in the season prior to his joining Blackpool, assisted them to finish runners-up to Doncaster Rovers for the championship of the Midland League. Said to be a quick and forceful tackler, he missed only three matches in his season at the Athletic Ground. In the close season he departed, along with goalkeeper Douglas, to join Warmley who were strengthening their ranks following their having won promotion to the First Division of the Southern League in 1897-98. Sadly the Warmley club failed to complete their first season in the higher division, being disbanded and wound up in February 1899.
Appearances: FL: 27 apps 0 gls FAC: 1 app 0 gls Total: 28 apps 0 gls

MARTIN, James 'Jimmy'
Inside forward
Born: Parkhead, circa 1876
Debut v Newton Heath (h) 17.10.96, won 4-2 (scored one goal)
CAREER: Airdrieonians. Bolton Wanderers March 1895. **Blackpool November 1895, registered for FL matches June 1896.** Walsall August 1898. Burton Wanderers May 1901 to cs 1902.

Jimmy Martin joined Blackpool in Lancashire League days, and when Football League status was achieved in 1896 he was second highest goal scorer in Blackpool's first League campaign with 10 goals in 23 matches. In the following season he appeared in every match but one and when first tried at centre forward in late January, a 3-2 away win against Small Heath impressed the selectors who retained him as attack leader for the remainder of the campaign. He next joined Walsall, at that time a Second Division club, and remained with them for three years, scoring 28 goals in 93 League matches and five in 10 FA Cup-ties. He left Fellows Park after Walsall lost their League status in 1901 and joined Burton United for one season in which he scored four goals in 28 Division Two matches
Appearances: 52 apps 17 gls FAC: 5 apps 0 gls Total: 57 apps 17 gls

MAYOR, Fred
Centre half back
CAREER: Blackpool 12th August 1898
Debut v Walsall (h) 10.9.98, lost 1-2

Centre half back Fred Mayor was just one of eight players who made just a single League appearance for Blackpool in the relegation season 1898-99. Despite a bright opening against Walsall, Jack Leadbetter scoring after just four minutes play, Walsall, inspired by their famous Wales international, Caesar August Llewelyn Jenkyns, fought back to win 2-1. In the following week, the Blackpool Club issued their balance sheet, revealing a loss on working of £441 2s. 5½"d. In the previous year they had lost £1,182 16s. Loss of League membership in the close season might well have been the end of Blackpool FC, but they spent only a season in the Lancashire League, amalagamated with the South Shore club, and were re-elected to the Second Division of the Football League on 25th May 1900.
Appearances: FL: 1 app 0 gls Total: 1 app 0 gls

METCALFE, Robert Simon
Inside left 5' 7½" 11st 8lbs
Born: Sunderland, 22nd May 1884
Died: Oakwood, Lowes Barn, Durham, 17th October 1950
Debut v Hull City (h) 2.9.11, won 3-2
CAREER: South Shields Parkside. **Blackpool May 1911.** Ashington January 1913. Houghton Rovers June 1913.

Discarded after appearing in the opening two fixtures of season 1911-12, inside forward Robert Metcalfe spent the rest of the season in reserve, until recalled for the final match of the season, a 4-0 defeat at Huddersfield Town. Considering the fact that Blackpool scored just 33 goals in 38 League matches, they were undebted to their defence, who kept their charge intact in twelve matches. In the close season, Metcalfe was transfer listed with a fee on his head. On appeal to the Football League, he was granted a free transfer. Initially employed as a chemist's assistant, the 1939 Census noted that he was employed as a pharmacist.
Appearances: FL: 3 apps 0 gls Total: 3 apps 0 gls

MILLER, Peter
Outside right
Born: Poulton
CAREER: Fleetwood Amateurs.
BLACKPOOL trial April 1903, amateur May 1903 to April 1906.
Debut v Gainsborough Trinity (a) 21.11.03, lost 1-3

Having played on trial for Blackpool Reserve against Accrington Stanley in Easter 1903, Peter Miller's capabilities were quickly seen, and the 'Fleetwood Express' reported as follows on his signing an amateur form in May 1903: "Advocates of local players will be pleased to hear that Peter Miller, a member of Fleetwood Amateurs' forward line last season, has signed for Blackpool." Sadly, as understudy to Billy Anderton, who missed only one first team match all season, Miller proved a capable player at reserve team level, but made only a trio of Second Division outings, the last of which was a 2-1 victory against Lincoln City on 16th January 1904.
Appearances: FL: 3 apps 0 gls Total: 3 apps 0 gls

MILLER, Peter Chippendale
Left full back
Born: Blackpool, 1st November 1883
Died: Wesham Park Hospital, Lancashire, 9th December 1963
Debut v Tottenham Hotspur (h) 10.10.08, drawn 1-1
CAREER: Fleetwood Amateurs. **Blackpool May 1908.** Fleetwood July 1910 to 1913.

With the normal full back pairing - captain Jack Scott and Sam Whittingham – both injured early in the season, Peter Miller was brought in from the Reserve to deputise in three consecutive matches in October. On his debut against the Spurs, 'Lloyd's Weekly' reported that the Blackpool rearguard of Fiske, Crewdson and Miller offered a defence that was all but perfect, as the Seasiders maintained their unbeaten run at Bloomfield Road. On what proved to be Miller's final League outing, a heavy 5-1 defeat at West Bromwich Albion ensued and the unfortunate full back was debited with an own goal. Peter Miller remained on Blackpool's register for a further two seasons, but did not get another

first team opportunity. He was later employed as a lithographic artist.
Appearances: FL: 3 apps 0 gls Total: 3 apps 0 gls

MILLER, Walter

Centre forward
5' 10½" 11st 10lbs
Born: Newcastle, October quarter 1882
Died: 1928
Debut v Manchester City (a) 2.9.09, won 2-1
CAREER: Wallsend Park Villa May 1904. Third Lanark. Newcastle East End August 1905. Ashington January 1906. Wallsend Park Villa May 1906. Sheffield Wednesday 1907. West Ham United May 1908. **Blackpool August 1909**. Third Lanark October 1910. Lincoln City May 1911. Merthyr Town January 1914. Dundee August 1914.

Walter Miller was given little opportunity with Sheffield Wednesday – three appearances and no goals – but he did rather better in a season with West Ham United, scoring five goals in 11 Southern League matches. Joining Blackpool, he scored three goals in his first four matches, but an injury early one caused him to miss five matches. A powerful centre forward, his game was marked by outstanding aerial ability, and a hard shot in either foot. He led the scoring list in his first season with 14 goals in 31 League matches, his tally including a hat trick on New Year's Day, in the 3-1 home win against Leeds City. He later assisted Lincoln City to win the Central League championship in 1911-12, scoring 20 goals in 27 matches.
Appearances: FL: 37 apps 15 gls FAC: 2 apps 0 gls

MILLERSHIP, Harry
Full back
5' 10½" 12st 0lbs
Born: Weston Rhyn, Chirk, 29th August 1889
Died: Blackburn, April quarter 1959
Debut v Huddersfield Town (a) 14.12.12, lost 0-3
CAREER: Castleford Town December 1908. Normanton November 1909. Fairburn United August 1910. Chirk 1910. Goole Town 1911. Fryston Colliery July 1912. **Blackpool October 1912**. (Wartime guest player with Rochdale November 1916 and Leeds City 1917-19) Leeds City August 1919. Rotherham County October 1919, fee £1,000. Barnsley September 1922, fee £350. Castleford Town September 1923.

Welsh international full back Harry Millership commenced in League football with Blackpool, getting his first opportunity following the transfer of Charlie Gladwin to Sunderland. He was a Leeds City player when League football recommenced after World War One, and when the club was wound up following the illegal payments scandal, a "£1,000 fee took him to Rotherham County, for whom he played in 81 games, scoring five goals. He made his international debut against England at Highbury in 1920, and played in all of Wales' international matches in 1920 and 1921. A final move in League circles brought only five appearances for Barnsley, and his career ended in the Yorkshire League with Castleford Town. After retiring from the game, he ran the Castle Hotel in Castleford and later worked at the Winter Gardens in Blackpool.
Appearances: FL: 30 apps 0 gls Total: 30 apps 0 gls
Honours: Wales International, 6 caps v England, Scotland & Ireland 1920 & 1921.

MILNE, William 'Bill'

Centre forward 5' 9½" 11st 7lbs
Born: Montrose, 21st February 1889
Died: Renfrewshire, 8th June 1973
Debut v Hull City (h) 2.9.11, won 3-2 (scored one goal)
CAREER: Montrose Rosevale. Montrose FC. Glossop May 1910. **Blackpool July 1911**. Aberdeen July 1912. Third Lanark May1913. Dundee May 1914.

Bill Milne commenced in League football as reserve centre forward to Harry Stapley, Glossop's crack amateur international marksman, and was afforded few opportunities, despite scoring on his debut. He had a great scoring record as a junior, was sturdily built, and shot well with either foot, but he did not always command a regular starting role with his other clubs. If there were deficiencies on his overall play, he lacked nothing as a goal scorer. With Blackpool he scored seven goals in 26 appearances, following with nine in 18 appearances for Aberdeen. Eight in 16 appearances for Third Lanark preceded his final spell in senior football with Dundee, where he failed to score in a single appearance.
Appearances: FL: 25 apps 6 gls FAC: 1 app 1 gl Total: 26 apps 7 gls

MITCHELL, James Frederick

Goalkeeper
6' 1" 13st 4lbs
Born: Waddington, near Clitheroe, 18th November 1895
Died: 4, Avenue Road, Leicester, 30th May 1975
Debut v Lincoln City (a) 20.3.15, drawn 0-0
CAREER: Arnold HouseGrammar School. Manchester University FC. **Blackpool amateur March 1915.** Northern Nomads. Manchester University. Preston North End October 1920. Manchester City May 1922. Leicester City October 1926. Stead & Simpson Works XI.

When Blackpool transferred Jimmy Kidd to Bolton Wanderers in March 1915, they gave a first team trial to amateur James Mitchell, a Manchester University student, who had made a very favourably impression one week earlier when he made his debut in a Central League match. The young and inexperienced goalkeeper gave early signs of talent beyond the ordinary as he conceded just one goal in his five appearances. Mitchell subsequently found fame in the 'Twenties not only for his goalkeeping but also because he played wearing spectacles. His game featured massive clearance kicks and athleticism; the latter underlined by his appearance for England in the 1920 Olympics, high jump event. Capped once by England and six times in Amateur Internationals, he appeared in 21 League matches for Preston North End and in 99 League matches for Manchester City. The son of a famous amateur billiards champion of 1894, for a time Mitchell was a master of his old school, later a director of the footwear chain, Stead & Simpson.
Appearances: FL: 5 apps 0 gls Total: 5 apps 0 gls
Honours: England Amateur International, 6 caps. Represented Great Britain in the 1922 Olympic Games at football and the high jump. England International, 1 cap 1925. (Preston North End) FA Cup finalist 1922

MITCHELL, Thomas 'Tommy'
Outside right 5' 8" 10st 7lbs
Born: Liversedge, *circa* 1892
Debut v Bradford Park Avenue (a) 6.2.12, drawn 0-0
CAREER: Liversedge. **Blackpool May 1911 to May 1912.**

In anticipation of the pending departure of Sid Hoad to Manchester City, Blackpool directors signed 19 year-old Tommy Mitchell, who was variously reported to have scored a total between 20 and 30 goals for Liversedge FC, members of the graphically named 'Yorkshire Heavy Woollen League' in 1910-11. When Blackpool's season got underway the

committee tried four different outside rights before introducing Mitchell for a run of three consecutive matches in the month of February 1912. Blackpool failed to score in the trio of matches, following the goalless encounter at Bradford, 1-0 defeats were sustained against Stockport County at home, and at Leeds City. Throughout the season Blackpool failed to score in 17 of their 38 League engagements, finishing with a total of 32 goals for the season. Only Gainsborough Trinity scored fewer, 30 goals, and they finished at the bottom of the Second Division and were not re-elected.
Appearances: FL: 3 apps 0 gls Total: 3 apps 0 gls

MORGAN, Hugh

Forward 5' 7" 11st 0lbs
Born: Shettleston, 7th August 1874
Died: 3111, Riverside Avenue, Somerset Centre, Bristol County, Massachusetts, USA, 4th June 1970.
Debut v Leicester Fosse (h) 3.9.04, drawn 0-0
CAREER: Harthill Thistle.Airdrieonians August 1896. Sunderland December 1896. Liverpool April 2nd to 23rd 1898. Bolton Wanderers February 1899, fee £200. Newton Heath December 1900. Manchester City August 1901. Accrington Stanley July 1902. **Blackpool May 1904 to June 1905**. Nelson October 1905. Hamilton Academical September 1906. North Wingfield St Lawrence (Derbyshire) August 1908. Reading September 1908. Pontypridd August 1912. Brentford August 1918. Philadelphia Field Club September 1921. Bethlehelm Steel. J & P Coates (Rhode Island) October 1922. Fall River Marksmen coach.

A fair-haired, energetic little forward, Hugh Morgan – a Scotsman with a Welsh-sounding name- began brightly in English football, playing in all but three matches for Sunderland in 1897-98 when they were runners up for the League championship. Transferred to Bolton Wanderers, who were struggling at the wrong end of Division One; despite scoring six goals in only 12 matches, Morgan's efforts failed to keep the Wanderers in the top flight. One season on, he helped them bounce straight back as runners up to Sheffield Wednesday. Then followed two indifferent seasons, with Newton Heath and Manchester City, who finished at the bottom of Division One. Two seasons of Lancashire Combination football with Accrington Stanley included a championship of Division One in 1902-03, and the runners up spot in 1903-04. On joining Blackpool, he scored the first of his goals against his former colleagues, netting twice in Blackpool's 4-1 win against Accrington Stanley in the third qualifying round of the FA Cup. Despite a good run in the Competition to the first round proper, and a 2-1 defeat at Bristol City of the First Division, League form had been disappointing throughout. Blackpool finished just one point above Stockport County, whose re-election application was unsuccessful. Hugh Morgan served with the RGA during World War One, and later with the Leicester Regiment.
Appearances: FL: 24 apps 4 gls FAC: 3 apps 3 gls Total: 27 apps 7 gls

MORLEY, Frederick 'Fred'

Inside/Outside right 5' 7½" 11st 7lbs
Born: Burslem, 1st March 1888
Died: 1970
Debut v Manchester City (a) 2.9.09, won 2-1
CAREER: Chesterton White Star. Reading September 1908. **Blackpool June 1909 to 1911**. Scunthorpe & Lindsey United October 1912. Goole Town June 1913. Clayton West United September 1913. Brentford 1913 to 1921. Philadelphia Field Club. J & P Coats (Rhode Island). Fall River Marksmen. J & P Coats (Rhode Island) again.

Versatile forward Fred Morley enjoyed his best season with Blackpool in 1910-11 when he took over the centre forward position with some success, being second highest scorer with 11 goals in 27 appearances, his total including a hat trick against Lincoln City in a 4-1 win in November. Throughout the season he received great support in a fairly settled front rank that lined up as follows: Hoad, A.Wolstenholme, Morley, Clennell and Cox. The seventh place finish was the best that Blackpool had achieved at that time, but without Clennell and Hoad for the following

season Blackpool scored only 32 goals in the 38 League matches, Fred Morley's contribution being two goals in 22 League outings. After a spell in non-League football, Morley joined Brentford, sampling Southern League and Football League action, in the latter he appeared in the Bees first Football League match against Exeter City. He ended his football career in USA, assisting three different clubs.
Appearances: FL: 81 apps 22 gls FAC: 3 apps 0 gls Total: 84 apps 22 gls

MORRIS, James John 'Jack'

Inside left
5' 8" 11st 4lbs
Born: Liscard, Wallasey, 11th February 1876
Died: Liverpool, 16th July 1947
Debut v Darwen (h) 31.3.99, won 6-0 (scored two goals)
CAREER: Liverpool South End. Rock Ferry F.C. May 1896. Liverpool South End June 1898. Rock Ferry F.C. South Liverpool July 1898. **Blackpool March 1899.** Notts County May 1900. Bristol City cs 1903. New Brompton May 1904. Accrington Stanley June 1905. **Blackpool June 1906.** Accrington Stanley October 1907. Egremont Social November 1908. Clitheroe Central September 1909. Hoylake March 1911. Burnell's Ironworks November 1911.

Jack Morris' first club after school days was Liverpool South End. He then joined Rock Ferry, who that season won the Liverpool Senior Cup, defeating the Everton Reserve team by two goals to one. His first sojourn with Blackpool (four goals in six matches) paved the way for his entry into First Division football with Notts County for whom he scored 33 goals in 82 League and Cup matches. He missed only three matches in a season with Bristol City, and he also won a Gloucester Senior Cup medal. With New Brompton, he missed just one Southern League match. Both Bristol City and New Brompton wished to retain him for another season, but Morris wanted to play football nearer to his home and signed for Accrington Stanley, who won the championship of the Lancashire Combination First Division with a seven-point lead over runners up, Darwen. In the summer he returned for a second spell with Blackpool in which he scored four goals in 18 League appearances. Jack Morris was a colourful character; he married three times and fathered seven children. In the 1920s he was a bookmaker and the proud owner of a Rolls Royce. In 1940 he moved his family to Solihull, where he worked in the Rover factory.
Appearances: FL: 24 apps 8 gls Total: 24 apps 8 gls.

MOSS, Samuel 'Sam'
Left half back
Born: Blackpool, 30th January 1879
Died: 1969
Debut v Blackburn Park Road, FAC 3Q (a) 3.11.00, won 1-0
CAREER: Poulton. **Blackpool July 1900.**

Reserve half back Sam Moss' only first team appearances were both English (FA) Cup-ties in season 1900-01. Blackpool were riding high in the Second Division, but after a narrow victory against Blackburn Park Road, which attracted a gate of 3,000 spectators to the Audley Hill Ground, this was followed by a 2-1 defeat at Darwen. The latter was considered a terrible downfall by Blackpool, leaders of the Second Division table at the time. The absence of Boulton, who was suffering from a family bereavement, and Threlfall, who had not recovered from an injury, made necessary a number of changes in the defence, Greenhalgh and Burden forming the back line, while Moss took Threlfall's place in the halves. 3,000 spectators packed in to the Anchor Ground and witnessed a thrilling encounter. Blackpool led after just five minutes through Harold Hardman, but Darwen replied two minutes later through Leaming, and on 15 minutes Cooper scored what proved to be the winning goal. In the League, Blackpool fell away after their excellent start, when they remained undefeated in the first eleven matches, finishing in a disappointing twelfth place in the table.
Appearances: FAC: 2 apps 0 gls Total: 2 apps 0 gls

MOUNT, Charles 'Charlie'
Outside left
Born: Cambuslang, 27th March1873
Died: Victoria Infirmary, Glasgow, 23rd May 1958
Debut v Lincoln City (a) 5.9.96, lost 1-3 (scored)
CAREER: Cambuslang Hibs. **Blackpool July 1896**. Cambuslang Hibs. Hibernian September 1897. St Mirren December 1897. Motherwell June 1898.

Charlie Mount scored from the left wing in each of his first three matches, and one in his final outing, a 3-1 home win against Lincoln City. Quite why that was the end of the story remains a mystery, as with a ratio of above a goal every other game he had more than realised expectations. Nevertheless he returned to Scotland and Whitefield Park before leaving Cumbuslang for a second time in a series of rapid moves in the 1897-98 season.
Appearances: FL: 9 apps 5 gls Total: 9 apps 5 gls

MUSGROVE, Charles
Centre forward
Debut v Burslem Port Vale (h) 14.4.06, won 2-1
CAREER: Blackpool amateur April 1906. Houghton Rangers June 1907. Wingate Albion August 1909.

A promising first appearance in the reserves against Chorley, when he was said to have played well and effected some accurate passing out to his partner on the wing, the amateur Robert Topping, resulted in Musgrave being handed his League debut against Burslem Port Vale, replacing Albert Brown, at inside-left. As the season drew to its conclusion, Musgrove held his place for three consecutive matches, within the space of three days. In addition to his debut, he figured in a 0-3 defeat at Leeds City and a 1-1 draw at Barnsley. He was not retained for the following season, and his early career and personal details remain untraced, although one report described him as: "A new importation from Scotland."
Appearances: FL: 3 apps 0 gls Total: 3 apps 0 gls

NESBITT, Robert 'Bert'Adam
Outside left 5' 7½" 11st 0lbs
Born: Embleton, Northumberland,, 22nd August 1884
Died: Northumberland, January quarter 1972
Debut v Hull City (h) 2.9.11, won 3-2 (scored one goal)
CAREER: Blyth Spartans May 1910. **Blackpool May 1911.**

When Blackpool sought a worthy successor to Jack Cox (q.v.) who had announced his intention to retire at the close of season 1911-12, Bert Nesbitt, described as a hard working outside left, was recruited from Blyth Spartans. In a promising start he netted Blackpool's first goal of the new season, and some five weeks later scored both of Blackpool's goals in the 2-1 away win at Stockport County. However, throughout the season, Jack Cox and Peter Quinn provided stiff competition for the left wing berth, despite Nesbitt's very respectable ratio of goals per game.
Appearances: FL: 11 apps 4 gls Total: 11 apps 4 gls

NIGHTINGALE, Arthur
Outside right
Debut v Gainsborough Trinity (a) 17.12.98, lost 0-7
CAREER: Blackpool November 1898 to 1900. Oswaldtwistle Rovers August 1908.

Arthur Nightingale's three senior appearances all came in relegation season 1898-99. In addition to his debut in the heavy 7-0 defeat at Gainsborough, his next outing was not much better – a 6-0 defeat at Walsall on 7th January. In the following week he was moved from the right wing to right half back for the home match against Burton Swifts, the 3-0 win being the best result recorded at the point. So, at least, he bowed out on a winning note. When Blackpool lost their Football League status and spent a season in the Lancashire League in 1899-1900, Arthur Nightingale remained in reserve, his name noted at right half in a 4-2 home win against White Star (Liverpool) on January 1900 However, his name did not appear on Blackpool's retained list for their return to Division Two in 1900-01, and his whereabouts remained a mystery until many

years later when the 'Lancashire Evening Post' reported his August 1908 move to Oswaldtwistle Rovers
Appearances: FL: 3 apps 0 gls Total: 3 apps 0 gls

NORRIS, Robert 'Bob'

Left half-back
5' 10" 11st 6lbs
Born: Preston, 17th July 1875
Died: Nottingham, 31st March 1940, age 64
Debut v Lincoln City (a) 5.9.96, lost 1-3
CAREER: South Shore F.C. April 1896. **Blackpool June 1896**. Nottingham Forest May 1898. Doncaster Rovers July 1904. Nottingham Forest trainer May 1905.

One of the best of Blackpool's early signings, and one of only two ever-present players in the club's first season in the Football League, Bob Norris coupled tenacious tackling with excellent distribution, and his form earned him a move to Nottingham Forest of the First Division in May 1898 when the'Nottingham Journal' heralded his arrival with the news that: "He has the virtue of being a total abstainer." His excellent form with Forest was rewarded with a place in an international trial match in March 1900, and later in the same month he played for the Football League against the Scottish League at Crystal Palace, when he had the misfortune to score an own goal in a 2-2 draw. In the following season, in an FA Cup-tie at Aston Villa, he fractured a leg and was sidelined for over a year. After six years at the City Ground, Norris spent a season with Doncaster Rovers, scoring three goals in 21 matches, before returning to Forest as trainer. He later became one of the best-known figures in local bowling circles, winning numerous competitions and representing the County. A licensed victualler, Bob Norris was for some years mine host at the Sir Richard Arkwright public house in Nottingham.
Appearances: FL: 52 apps 1 gl FAC: 4 apps 1 gl Total: 56 apps 2 gls
Honours: Football League representative, one appearance 1900.

O'CONNOR, Peter
Centre forward
Debut v Darwen (a) 12.9.96, won 3-2
CAREER: Durham County. **Blackpool August 1896**. Bacup October to December 1896. Stanley F.C. August 1897.

Peter O'Connor was first introduced as: "A big, upstanding lad, endowed with dash, and with ever an eye for the main chance." In the first Football League fixture played at the Raikes Hall Ground against Burton Wanderers, he scored the first goal in the 5-0 win. For the second half, Jack Parkinson was switched to centre forward, Connor moving to the left wing. His first appearance in the new position was marked by his unfairly tackling an opponent "calling upon his head the wrath of the referee" according to one match report. After a run of four consecutive matches it became apparent that although he got through a lot of work he was largely ineffective and was released to join Bacup in early October. Despite scoring two of Bacup's four goals against Nantwich on his debut, he failed to hold his place in the side and was released in December of the same season.
Appearances: FL: 4 apps 1 gl Total: 4 apps 1 gl

OWEN, Alfred Sydney 'Syd'

Winger
5' 11" 11st 0lbs
Born: Tunstall, 30th August 1885
Died: Blackpool, 22nd August 1925
Debut v Fulham (a) 23.9.11, lost 0-3
CAREER: An amateur throughout with North Staffs Nomads. Northern Nomads. Stoke January 1907. Stockport County July1907. Burslem Port Vale October 1907. Everton 1907. Stoke April 1908. Burslem Port Vale September 1908. Leicester Fosse October 1908. Shrewsbury Town June 1909. Newcastle Town. Northern Nomads. **Blackpool amateur May 1911**. Stoke November 1912. Halesowen Town December 1912. Ironbridge November 1913.

On recruiting the services of the noted amateur Syd Owen, secretary of the Players'

Union, it was expected that he would prove a worthy successor to Jack Cox, in the final season of his outstanding career. Sadly, after just two League outings, one on the right wing and one on the left, he spent the remainder of his days at Bloomfield Road in the Central League side. Owen's best spell in League football came with Leicester Fosse – 51 League and Cup appearances and 13 goals. He was selected for an Amateur Internation trial match at Anfield in January 1910 and scored once in the Whites v Stripes fixture but subsequently failed to win a full cap. A chartered accountant by profession, he took up a business appointment in Budapest on 1913, and later enlisted, serving in turn with the North Staffordshires, the Grenadier Guards and the Northamptonshire Regiment.
Appearances: FL: 2 apps 0 gls Total: 2 apps 0 gls

OWERS, Ebenezer Fuller 'Ginger'
Centre forward 5' 10" 11st 4lbs
Born: Leytonstone, 21st October 1888
Died: Chigwell, Essex, 16th May 1964
Debut v Stockport County (a) 2.9.07, drawn 1-1
CAREER: Leytonstone & District Schools. Bashford 1904. Leytonstone 1905. Leyton December 1906. **Blackpool May 1907.** West Bromwich Albion November 1907. Chesterfield Town January 1909. Bristol City June 1910. Darlington June 1911. Bristol City March 1912. Clyde March 1913. Celtic (loan) December 1913. Clyde May 1914.

A bright start to his brief stay at Bloomfield Road included two goals in a 5-0 win against Clapton Orient on his second appearance, and although he failed to score in his penultimate game against West Bromwich Albion, in the same month Owers was transferred to the Hawthorns club. Fortunately, on this occasion, Blackpool had a ready-made substitute for his position in the amateur William Grundy who netted 13 goals in 26 matches. Owers meanwhile had few opportunities with his new club (four League matches) and on moving to Chesterfield Town his three goals in 15 matches was insufficient to keep them in Division Two. In the following season, however, a goal storm from Owers took Chesterfield to the championship of the Midland League, his remarkable record being 40 goals in 41 matches. The Chesterfield club failed to gain immediate re-election to the Second Division, and Owers moved on to Bristol City. Despite his return of 16 goals in 31 matches City were relegated from Division One. He moved on to Darlington of the North Eastern League and had scored 19 goals for them – including a hat trick against Carlisle United and four against Jarrow – when Bristol City recalled him. A further year at Ashton Gate took his overall totals to 32 goals in 62 matches. The final stages of his career were spent in Scotland, with a loan to Celtic the highlight. His 10 goals in 13 League matches helped Celtic to the championship of the Scottish League, and they also won the Scottish Cup, after a replay. Ebenezer, however, was dropped after appearing in the first meeting with Hibernian, who were defeated 4-1 in the replay. During the First World War Owers served with the 23rd Footballer's Battalion and the Royal Fusileers. He was wounded and discharged in October 1917 as unfit for military service.
Appearances: FL: 9 apps 3 gls Total: 9 apps 3 gls

PAGNAM, Frederick 'Fred'

Outside right, later centre forward
5' 9" 12st 0lbs
Born: Poulton-le-Fylde, 4th September 1891
Died: Salmesbury, near Preston, 1st March 1962
Debut v Stockport County (a) 12.4.13, lost 0-2
CAREER: Poulton Grammar School. Birchall Boys Club. Lytham. Blackpool Wednesday. Huddersfield Town June 1910. Doncaster Rovers July 1912. Southport Central January 1913. **Blackpool February 1913.** Gainsborough Trinity. Liverpool May 1914. (Wartime guest player with Arsenal, Blackpool, Lytham, Belfast Celtic and Liverpool) Arsenal October 1919, fee £1,500). Cardiff City March 1921, fee £3,000. Watford December 1921, fee £1,000, player-manager from May 1926 to June 1929. Blyth Primrose. Blyth Plessey Athletic. Blyth Spartans December 1930. Galatasary coach

July 1931 to June 1932. Turkey FA national coach July 1931. HVV Netherlands assistant-coach 1933. DWV Netherlands coach 1934. Montpellier coach 1934. FC Haarlem coach 1937 to May 1940. De Volewijckers part time coach 1938.

The son of a Blackpool bank manager, Fred Pagnam returned to the Blackpool district in late season 1912-13, after earlier departing to play for Huddersfield Town, Doncaster Rovers and Southport Central. He left Southport when the club's directors offered all their players a wage cut or a free transfer. He arrived at Bloomfield Road too late to have the opportunity to play in many League games, but was more regularly employed in 1913-14, despite a strong challenge from John Charles for the right wing position. Placed on the transfer list with a fee of £75 on his head, on the player's appeal to the Football League, the fee was reduced to £25, an absolute bargain for the Liverpool club where he became noted as a prolific goal scorer from centre forward, netting 28 goals in 37 League matches. A series of big money transfers followed, firstly to Arsenal (26 goals in 50 League matches), then to Cardiff City (eight goals in 27 matches) and finally to Watford (67 goals in 144 matches). A lengthy spell of coaching overseas came to an abrupt end when he fled the Nazis, along with his Dutch wife in 1940. He was later engaged in the licenced trade in Lancashire.
Appearances: FL: 22 apps 1 gl Total: 22 apps 1 gl

PARKINSON, John 'Jack' Arnold

Centre forward/Centre half back
Born: Blackpool, 27th August 1874
Died: Blackpool, 20th December 1911
Debut v Lincoln City (a) 5.9.96, lost 1-3
CAREER: South Shore August 1895. **Blackpool June 1896**. Liverpool May 1899. **Blackpool again August 1900 to 1909**. Barrow player manager January 1910.

Commencing as inside or centre forward, Jack Parkinson led Blackpool's scoring list with 12 goals in 27 matches in their first season as a Football League club. He left for a season with Liverpool when Blackpool lost their League status in 1899-1900, but returned when they were re-elected after just one season in the Lancashire League. One match report from his first season, and a 4-2 win against Newton Heath, ran as follows: "Parkinson was a treat in the centre, knitting his wings together finely, passing accurately and shooting with great judgment and strength, while his two goals were beauties." A move to centre half in season 1903-04 extended his career, as he was 34 years of age when he commenced his final season. Summer months were always spent following his occupation as a boatman, and he always reported for pre-season training with a healthy tan on his face. Among many offers for his signature, Sheffield United were anxious to secure his services following his memorable display in the February 1906 Cup-tie which captivated the home supporters. Two Southern League clubs were also anxious to secure him at the beginning of the same season, but failed to persued him to leave his native parts. Sadly, his death came in tragic circumstances when he was badly scalded in heroically rescuing an assistant from a tank of boiling sea water at the Corporation Baths, of which establishment he was appointed superintendent only a few months earlier. He was only 37 years of age, and was to have been recommended by the Corporation to the Carnegie Hero Fund.
Appearances: FL: 365 apps 52 gls FAC: 29 apps 3 gls Total: 394 apps 55 gls

PARKINSON, Robert 'Bob'
Centre-forward
5' 9" 12st 0lbs
Born: Preston, 27th April 1873
Debut v Lincoln City (a) 5.9.96, lost 1-3
CAREER: Preston Ramblers. Preston Athletic. Fleetwood Rangers. Rotherham Town December 1894. Luton Town May 1895. **Blackpool June 1896 and re-signed March 1902**. Warmley August 1897. Nottingham Forest October 1898. Newton Heath November 1899. Watford November 1900. Swindon Town cs 1901.

Bob Parkinson was at inside left in Blackpool's first-ever Football League match, but he did not hold his place in the side, despite being tried in four of the five forward positions within the space of nine appearances. He next spent a season as captain of Warmley who won 19 of their 22 Southern League matches, scoring 108 goals and conceding just 15. Despite this outstanding record they were pipped by one point by Royal Artillery (Portsmouth) for the League title. He became the third ex-Blackpool player to join Nottingham Forest, but made only two League appearances before joining Newton Heath for whom he scored seven goals in 15 matches, but was transfer-listed in March 1900 following a suspension. In 15 Southern League matches for Watford he netted five goals, but did not appear at first team level for his final club, Swindon Town.
Appearances: FL: 8 apps 1 gl FAC: 1 app 1 gl Total: 9 apps 2 gls

PARR, Henry 'Harry'

Full back
Born: Blackpool, 18th April 1868
Died: Blackpool, April quarter1944
Debut v Lincoln City (a) 5.9.96, lost 1-3
CAREER: Blackpool St John's. **Blackpool June 1896, and re-signed November 1902.**

Harry Parr's association with the Blackpool club began at 17 years of age. At an even earlier age he played for Blackpool St John's, a noted club for both cricket and football in those days. He was a regular, along with elder brother Tom, with several season's experience when he made his Football League debut at the age of 28. Rarely absent at right full back for the first three seasons in Division Two, and for one season in the Lancashire League following relegation, he then decided to retire. Two years later, when he found his old club in a dilemma, he readily agreed to turn out once more and appeared in two matches spanning November and December 1902. Press reports confirmed that: "There is still something of the old warhouse in him," but Harry Parr admitted that he would have done better if he had had the benefit of a few more days in training.
Appearances: FL: 87 apps 2 gls FAC: 5 apps 0 gls Total: 92 apps 2 gls

PEARSON, Alfred 'Alf'
Centre half back 6' 0" 12st 0lbs
Born: Halliwell, Bolton, April quarter 1886 (Baptised 4th July 1886)
Died: Litherland Canal, Sefton, 25th June 1911
Debut v Bradford City (a) 3.11.06, lost 0-3
CAREER: St Helens Town. **Blackpool May 1906**. Rossendale United September 1908.

On signing for Blackpool, the 'Fleetwood Express' reported: "Pearson, the centre half back of St Helens Town, is considered one of the best in the Lancashire Combination, and he played a particularly fine game recently at Blackpool. He is young, having not yet reached his majority." He received his first opportunity when Jack Parkinson was sidelined with a sprained leg muscle, and held his place for four consecutive matches. Pearson was re-signed for 1907-08, but added just one further League outing to his tally, a 3-0 defeat at Fulham on 14th December, and moved on to Rossendale United. Originally employed as a cotton spinner, by 1911 he was a Police Constable with the Lancaster Force. He had married Hannah Farrimond on 10th June of that year in Bolton, and tragically died some two weeks later in the Litherland Canal, Sefton, being drowned while trying to save a suicidal woman.
Appearances: FL: 5 apps 0 gls Total: 5 apps 0 gls

PENTLAND, Frederick 'Fred' Beaconsfield

Forward
5' 9" 12st 0lbs
Born: Wolverhampton, 29th July 1883
Died: Lytchett Matrayers, Dorset, 16th March 1962
Debut v Woolwich Arsenal (a) 5.9.03, lost 0-3
CAREER: Avondale Juniors. Willenhall Swifts. Small Heath August 1900. **Blackpool June 1903.** Blackburn Rovers October 1903.

Brentford May 1906. Queens Park Rangers May 1907. Middlesbrough June 1908, fee £350 Halifax Town player-manager February 1913. Stoke May 1913. Halifax Town December 1913. Coached the German Olympic team May 1914, and at the outbreak of World War One he was interned for the duration. AS Strasburg (France) manager-coach 1919. French Olympic team assistant trainer 1920. Real Racing Club de Santander (Spain) coach 1921. Athletic Bilbao (Spain) manager-coach 1922. Club Atletico de Madrid (Spain) 1925. Real Oviedo (Spain) 1926. Club Atletico Madrid (Spain) 1927. Atletico Bilbao (Spain) 1929. Spain national team coach May 1929. Club Atletico de Madrid (Spain) 1929. Athletic Bilbao (Spain) 1933. Brentford assistant manager 1936-37. Barrow manager January 1938 to June 1940.

Dash, pace, and skill on the ball brought five goals in just eight matches for Blackpool, form that did not go unnoticed, and Fred Pentland made the first of his many moves to Blackburn Rovers after just six months at Bloomfield Road. He became immensely popular with the Blackburn supporters, and when he signed for Brentford in May 1906, had a remarkable send-off from the town. A crowd of players and friends occupied the station platform, and, led by the Palace Theatre Band, sang "Auld Lang Syne" and "He's a jolly good fellow". Two years in Southern League football followed in the second of which his 15 goals in 37 matches took Queens Park Rangers to the Southern League championship, they also drew with Football League champions, Manchester United, in the inaugural Charity Shield Final match at Stamford Bridge. Further success followed with Middlesbrough for whom he appeared in 96 League and Cup matches, scoring 11 goals. It was during his spell at Ayresome Park that Fred Pentland won his five England caps, on each occasion finishing on the winning side. The timing of his move to Germany to take up his first coaching appointment in May 1914 was unfortunate as he was then quickly interned for the duration. When hostilities ended he worked briefly in France but his greatest success came in Spanish football, as outlined below. The son of a former Lord Mayor of Birmingham who gave his son the unusual middle name of Beaconsfield, due to his admiration of Benjamin Disraeli, Earl of Beaconsfield.
Appearances: FL: 8 apps 5 gls Total: 8 apps 5 gls
Honours: England International, 5 caps (All victories). Honours Abroad: Copa Del Rey winner, five times. Campeonatode Vicayo winner, six times. Spanish League Championship, twice.

PICKFORD, Percy
Left half back
Born: Macclesfield, 20th July 1879
Died: Parkside Hospital, Macclesfield, 11th January 1957
Debut v Woolwich Arsenal (a) 5.9.03, lost 0-3
CAREER: Macclesfield amateur. Stockport County April 1900. **Blackpool August 1903.** Macclesfield September 1905. Burslem Port Vale June 1906. Macclesfield September 1907, remaining until season 1913-14.

Percy Pickford commenced with his hometown club, Macclesfield, but spent the best part of his career with Stockport County, whom he assisted to the championship of the Lancashire League in his first season. Election to the Second Division of the Football League followed in 1900-01, but he departed after three successive re-election applications, during which time he had appeared in 59 League matches and six FA Cup-ties. He scored just one goal, at Chesterfield Town on 19th April 1902, four Stockport players missed their train to Chesterfield and they took to the field with only seven players, in the circumstances 'only' an 8-1 defeat was quite an achievement. With Blackpool, Pickford made just one first team appearance, a 0-3 defeat by Woolwich Arsenal at Plumstead. Staying in London after their defeat, a friendly match was played on the Monday evening against Ilford FC. This was won 3-0, Threlfall, Pentland and Adams (own goal) the scorers. In 1911 Percy Pickford was employed as a silk designer in Macclesfield, and in 1939 was listed as a textile designer, living at 89, Crompton Road, Macclesfield.
Appearances: FL: 1 app 0 gls Total: 1 app 0 gls

POWNALL, James 'Jim'
Outside left 5' 8" 11st 2lbs
Born: Hoyland 22nd September 1888
Died: Birdwell, Barnsley, 11th February 1966
Debut v Leicester Fosse (h) 28.10.11, drawn 1-1
CAREER: Rotherham County. **Blackpool May 1910, and re-signed April 1911.**

Jim Pownall's one senior appearance against Leicester Fosse brought the following observation from the Leicester Mercury's correspondent; "For the first half of the game against Fosse, Pownall, who was making his debut at outside-left, played brilliantly. Later, however, he fell to pieces, and in this week's eleven is replaced by Bradshaw." Presumably lacking the necessary stamina to last for the full 90 minutes, he did not get another opportunity, despite being re-signed for 1910-11.
Appearances: FL: 1 app 0 gls Total: 1 app 0 gls

PRATT, Thomas Peet
Inside forward
Born: Fleetwood, 28th August 1873
Died: Fleetwood, 22nd November 1935
Debut v Manchester United (h) 25.3.05, lost 0-1
CAREER: Fleetwood Rangers. Grimsby Town June 1895. Preston North End June 1896, re-signed April 1897. Tottenham Hotspur April 1899. Preston North End May 1900. Fleetwood. Preston North End June 1901. Woolwich Arsenal 1903. Fulham May 1904. **Blackpool March 1905**. Fleetwood. **Blackpool February 1907.**

The 'Fleetwood Express' reported as follows when Tom Pratt joined Blackpool for the second time in February 1907: "It will be remembered that Tom Pratt, the Fleetwood player, joined Blackpool towards the end of the last season but one, and was instrumental in Blackpool retaining their Division Two status. Although he has not been playing much lately, he has slimmed down considerably. His weight problems were thought to mark his decline, however, he is now as physically fit for playing as he ever was, being quite two stone lighter than when he last played for Blackpool. If he can only get himself fully match fit, he should again be a power of good for Blackpool, because his dashing style and powerful shooting is just what Blackpool have lacked this season." Sadly, however, what amounted to a trial at Bloomfield Road was not extended. In earlier days, highlights included a Southern League championship win with Tottenham Hotspur, which happily coincided with their first season at their new ground at White Hart Lane. Tom Pratt led the scoring list with 25 goals in 30 matches, including successive hat tricks in three matches in February 1900. His overall Football League record amounted to 189 matches and 62 goals. With Preston North End, in three separate spells, he totalled 134 matches and 43 goals. By occupation he was a motor engineer.
Appearances: FL: 8 apps 2 gls Total: 8 apps 2 gls

QUINN, Peter, MM and bar

Outside-left
5' 7½" 11st 0lbs
Born: Sunderland, 3rd December 1888
Died: Blackpool, 27th February 1976
Debut v Hull City (h) 10.12.10, won 2-0
CAREER: Bankhead Albion 1908. Spennymoor United 1909. **Blackpool December 1910.** (Wartime guest player with Sunderland Rovers, Fulham & Everton). Preston North End March 1920, fee £3,000. Fleetwood July 1921. Bury January 1923, fee £1,125. New Brighton July 1923 to May 1924. Bankhead Albion.

An instance of Peter Quinn's ardent enthusiasm for the game was afforded at the outset of his career with Blackpool. He was signed by the club on Thursday, and travelled to Blackpool on Friday. On Saturday he played against Northern Nomads, on Monday against Everton Reserves, on Wednesday against Bury, and was included in the team for the following Saturday – certainly a brisk introduction to life in the Football League! Both Blackpool teams opened season 1911-12 with a win. Quinn scoring two goals in the

Reserves 3-0 win at Burnley. Some three months later, representatives from Burnley were at Blackpool watching Quinn play with the Reserves. The Blackpool committee came to an agreement to transfer Quinn to Burnley for a sum of £200. Quinn, however, refused to go to Turf Moor, and the bargain was at an end. The 'Northern Daily Telegraph Annual 1912-13' reported as follows: "One of Blackpool's most popular forwards, hails from Spennymoor, and won distinction in the North-Eastern League before he joined the Seasiders. He is about 22 years of age, and has done splendid service for Blackpool during the past two seasons in both inside positions. He shows promise of developing into quite a class player." His first real opportunity came in 1911-12, with Jack Cox out of the team so often, and, figuring in 29 games, showed himself to be a clever dribbler and shot. Peter Quinn assisted Blackpool at either side of the Great War, in which he served with distinction, returning with a Military Medal and bar. While in France he played in the English Military team which had a splendid run of success. On joining Preston North End, he assisted them to avoid relegation from the top flight in his first season at Deepdale and went on to record a century of League and Cup matches, including his appearance in the 1922 FA Cup Final, won 1-0 by Huddersfield Town. It was thought that his career was over when he suffered a broken leg during his brief spell with Bury, but he recoverd to become New Brighton's first goal scorer in the Football League, and as one journalist noted: "One could see the old head in his work." Quinn's 30 appearances and two goals for the Rakers took his career aggregate figures to 275 League matches and 29 goals.
Appearances: FL: 154 apps 16 gls FAC: 9 apps 0 gls Total: 163 apps 16 gls
Honours: Preston North End, FA Cup finalists 1922.

RAISBECK, Luke

Half back
5' 8½" 11st 7lbs
Born: Wallacestone near Polmont, Stirling, 2nd September 1878
Died: Windsor, Ontario, Canada, 31st May 1967
Debut v Burton United (h) 2.9.05, won 2-0
CAREER: Airdrieonians July 1897. Motherwell April 1898. Royal Albert July 1898. Slamannan November 1898. Sheffield United March 1899. Third Lanark August 1899. Middlesbrough October 1899. West Ham United June 1900. Falkirk May 1901. Clyde February 1902. Port Glasgow Athletic May 1904. Brynn Central July 1904. **Blackpool May 1905.** Carlisle United May 1906. Lancaster October 1907. Ashton Town August 1909. Barrow October 1909.

Born into a footballing family, Luke Raisbeck's brothers Andrew (Hull City) and William (Sunderland and Derby County) were outshone by first cousin Alexander (Six Scottish caps and over 300 appearances for Liverpool). Luke meantime followed a wandering path through Scottish and English football, but recorded only 37 League appearances in total – 19 for Middlesbrough in addition to his Blackpool return of 18. Off the field, in May 1905, he was sued for damages amounting to £500, for alleged breach of promise by Mary Richards of Kelvinhaugh, Glasgow. In the following month Luke married Martha Fearnley in Glasgow, and in November of the same year the case against him was not proven, due to the court's lack of success in locating the persuer. Luke later emigrated and was naturalized in Elmo, West Virginia.
Appearances: FL: 18 apps 0 gls Total: 18 apps 0 gls

READ, William Henry 'Harry'

Outside right
5' 9" 10st 7lbs
Born: Blackpool, 1st October 1885
Died: Blackpool, April quarter 1951
Debut v Grimsby Town (a) 26.10.07, drawn 2-2 (scored one goal)
CAREER: Junior football to Preston North End as an amateur. **Blackpool amateur 1906, professional May 1907**. Colne August 1909. Sunderland April 1910. Chelsea May 1911. Dundee March 1913. Swansea Town 1914. Chesterfield Municipal.

Harry Read's career got off to a shaky start when he was suspended by the committee of the Fylde and District Amateur League for six weeks from 5th November 1906, having signed registration papers for two different clubs. At the special meeting it was also decided that Read would still be considered a Blackpool Combination player; also that the Lytham club be fined 5 shillings for playing Read, who was not eligible, in a cup-tie on 6th October 1906. About a year later he made his Football League debut and scored against Grimsby Town. After two seasons, the last of which found Blackpool on the bottom of Division Two, he joined Colne and was second highest scorer with 11 goals when transferred to Sunderland for whom he made four appearances and scored two goals. In similar fashion he appeared just four times for both Chelsea and Dundee. A move to Swansea Town, of the Southern League, was marked by the Swans' remarkable run in the FA Cup, with a 1-0 win against League champions Blackburn Rovers, and a battling draw at Newcastle United in round two, followed, disappointingly, by a 2-0 defeat in the replay at the Vetch. Harry Read served as a Lance Corporal in the Coldstream Guards in World War One and later went to Canada to become a farmer but returned to live in Clayton-le-Moors. The 1939 Census revealed that he was living in Blackpool and working as a shellfish merchant on his own account.

Appearances: FL: 30 apps 3 gls FAC: 1 app 0 gls Total: 31 apps 3 gls

REEVES, George William

Forward
5' 6" 10st 7lbs
Born: Sutton-in-Ashfield, July 1884
Died: Sutton-in-Ashfield, 15th May 1962
Debut v Nottingham Forest (h) 8.3.13, won 2-1
CAREER: Blackwell Road Church School. Sutton-in-Ashfield. Blackwell Colliery. Sutton Town January 1902. Sutton-in-Ashfield. Ripley Athletic May 1904. Sutton Town June 1906. Barnsley December 1906, fee £50. Aston Villa November 1907, fee £1,000. Bradford Park Avenue November 1909. **Blackpool March 1913.** New Hucknall Colliery June 1913.

George Reeves earned the Barnsley club a handsome profit on their £50 outlay after he had netted 27 goals in just 30 League appearances including hat tricks against Fulham and the Wolves in 1907-08. Sadly, his dream move to Aston Villa was blighted by a bad knee injury, but he still managed to score 11 goals in 35 matches before joining Bradford Park Avenue for whom he scored 22 goals in 63 League and Cup appearances, additionally winning a West Riding Senior Cup medal in November 1910. Blackpool was his last port of call in terms of senior football, and while it was felt that his experience would be of help to Blackpool's young forward line, he set the worst possible example, being suspended sine die for inattention to training orders. Reeves' mother, Sarah, was unmarried and George was brought up by the Adlington family, based in Huthwaite. As acknowledgement he became known as George William Adlington Reeves, but was always known as just "George".
Appearances: FL: 3 apps 0 gls Total: 3 apps 0 gls

REILLY, James Henry
Left full back/Outside left
Born: Prestwich, Manchester, October quarter 1885
Debut v Lincoln City (h) 22.4.05, won 1-0
CAREER: Sale Holmefield. **Blackpool amateur February 1905.** Brynn Central January 1906. Salford United. Sale Holmefield November 1906. Hyde June 1907. Berry's Association November 1907. Hooley Hill November 1908. Rusholme September 1909.

A 'Lancashire Evening Post' report on a Blackpool Reserve team match against Hyde in April 1905 ran as follows: "Owing to Jones being drafted into the League side, the Blackpool eleven was rearranged and instead of Reilly playing at full back, where he had been all along, he was put to outside right. He had played there before, but not for Blackpool, so that his success in the role was most surprising. It was due to him that four goals were scored by Blackpool, and the spectators were very enthusiastic about him. It seems very likely that he will next appear in the League team." He did in fact make two late season senior appearances, at outside right on his debut against Lincoln City, and, two days later he was at outside left at Manchester United. He remained on Blackpool's register for the following season but added only one more League outing to his total, in a 3-0 home defeat against West Bromwich Albion on 4th November 1905.
Appearances: FL: 3 apps 0 gls Total: 3 apps 0 gls

RIMMER, Hugh

Right full back
Born: Fleetwood, January quarter 1881
Died: Fleetwood, 5th August 1926
Debut v Chelsea (h) 8.9.06, drawn 0-0
CAREER: Fleetwood Amateurs. **Blackpool July 1906.** Nelson May 1908 to May 1915.

Hugh Rimmer joined Blackpool following an excellent season with Fleetwood Amateurs in 1905-06. He progressed well in the Combination side alongside Alf Pearson and Bert Wake, the trio being considered the best of Blackpool's junior players. He held a first team place for several weeks in the following season, appearing at right full back in 14 League matches. A move to Nelson, along with John Gow, proved to be an excellent move by the Seedhill club, particularly in the case of Hugh Rimmer who became the mainstay of Nelson' rearguard for seven seasons and captain of the team from 1909-10 onwards. Described as: "A clean, gentlemanly, and polished defender." He led the Light Blues to their best season in 1912-13 when they finished in third place in the First Division of the Lancashire Combination. He was employed as a builder's joiner when not playing football.
Appearances: FL: 21 apps 0 gls Total: 21 apps 0 gls

ROBSON, William

Right full back
5' 10½" 12st 0lbs
Born: Gateshead
Debut v Huddersfield Town (a) 27.9.13, lost 0-1
CAREER: Blackpool June 1913.

Blackpool signed two new full backs in preparation for the 1913-14 season. William

Robson, described as a sturdy and resolute defender, accompanied Albert Tulloch from the North East to Bloomfield Road, and it was Robson who first made the breakthrough into the League eleven, providing a strong challenge to Harry Millership for the right back berth. In his second season, a switch from right to left full back, to cover for the injured Jimmy Jones, provided the first opportunity for Tulloch, who had spent his first season in the Central League eleven.
Appearances: FL: 46 apps 0 gls FAC: 2 apps 0 gls Total: 48 apps 0 gls

ROOKE, John
Inside right
Born: Bitton, Gloucester, October quarter 1878
Died: Kingswood, Bristol, 10th July 1938
Debut v Woolwich Arsenal (a) 5.9.03, lost 0-3
CAREER: **Blackpool June 1903.** Bristol East August 1904. Staple Hill September 1906. Kingswood Rovers September 1909.

John Rooke was once described as; "A good worker, who mainly took the role of a provider." Certainly his goal return was modest in a season when Blackpool sold their best forward, Fred Pentland, after he had netted five goals in nine matches. It took John Rooke 25 matches to reach the same total, but his two goals in the season's penultimate fixture at Bradford City ensured that the Seasiders moved narrowly clear of the bottom three places in the table, and a re-election application. In 1911 John Rooke was living in Kingswood, Bristol, and working as a clicker in the boot and shoe industry
Appearances: FL: 21 apps 5 gls FAC: 2 apps 0 gls Total: 23 apps 5 gls

ROOKS, William 'Billy'

Utility 5' 7½" 11st 6lbs
Born: Grangetown near Sunderland, 14th December 1890
Died: Ashton-under-Lyne, 14th December 1972
Debut v Bradford Park Avenue (h) 20.12.13, won 2-1
CAREER: Willington. Sunderland Rovers November 1912. Manchester City (trial) April 1913. **Blackpool May 1913**. (Wartime guest player with Sunderland Rovers) Accrington Stanley July 1922. Hurst player-manager May 1927. Great Harwood September 1929. Hurst committee June 1930; Secretary to 1956 and groundsman 1957.

Billy Rooks was a live-wire performer who obviously enjoyed his football and was prepared to play in any position. He began with Blackpool as an outside left, but eventually evolved as a utility defender, his one hundred-plus appearances rewarded with a benefit of £300. He was appointed captain on transferring to Accrington Stanley, but a cartilage operation restricted him to just 13 matches in his first season. He spent the follow season at centre half, and in 1924-25 alternated between wing half and full back. It was a continuing pattern, for in the course of his five seasons with Stanley he played in every outfield defensive positions and even had the odd game at centre forward. In recognition of his services Rooks was awarded a benefit match in May 1927. A Reds v Blues match included in both teams players from Blackburn Rovers, Blackpool and Preston North End.
Appearances: FL: 103 apps 4 gls FAC: 7 apps 0 gls Total: 110 apps 4 gls
Representative honour: Central League v Lancashire Combination at Tranmere 25th April 1921.

ROSE, Frederick Arnold
Centre half back 5' 10½" 12st 0lbs
Born: Charlton 19th February 1881
Died: 1960
Debut v Gainsborough Trinity (a) 28.9.07, lost 1-2
CAREER: Tunbridge Wells Rangers. **Blackpool May 1907.**

Despite winning their first home match of season 1907-08, by 5-0 against Clapton Orient, Blackpool supporters then had to wait three months for a second win, 4-3 against Lincoln City on 7th December. Between times, the directors had tried numerous line-ups in the hope of finding a winning combination. Fred Rose, signed as understudy to Parkinson for the centre half berth, failed to make his mark when Parkinson was injured in mid

term, his single appearance in the centre of defence coming on Christmas Day at Burnley in a 2-1 defeat before an attendance estimated at 12,000.
Appearances: FL: 3 apps 0 gls Total: 3 apps 0 gls

RUSHTON, Frank

Right full back
5' 6" 10st 0lbs
Born: Blackburn, 19th September 1893
Died: Preston, 4th April 1970
Debut v Bristol City (a) 15.11.13, lost 0-1
CAREER: Hamilton Central. **Blackpool amateur 1st April, professional 30th April 1913.** Barry Dock. Caerphilly 1920. Chorley August 1922. Darwen 1924. Clitheroe.

Hardly the build for a full back, Frank Rushton nevertheless showed enough promise in Central League matches to warrant his being retained until enlistment in the East Lancashire Territorial Force, and in 1915 as a driver in the RHA. Originally employed as a cloth looker (examiner) in a local weaving mill, he was later proprietor of the Riverside Café in Preston.
Appearances: FL: 1 app 0 gls Total: 1 app 0 gls

SANDERSON, Thomas 'Tommy'
Inside left 5' 8"
Born: Chorley, 3rd August 1880
Died: Blackpool, October quarter 1946
Debut v Grimsby Town (h) 7.3.06, won 2-0 (scored one goal)
CAREER: Freehold Athletic. Chorley St George December 1903. Swindon Town March 1904. Southern United May 1905. **Blackpool March 1906.** Carlisle United May 1906. Chorley August 1910. Carlisle United October 1910 to at least November 1919.

Tommy Sanderson joined Swindon Town in March 1904 on wages of £1.50 per week and scored 33 goals for their Reserve team. The Swindon club sent a £5 donation to his former club, Chorley St George, as a thank you for his services. Despite a scoring debut for Blackpool he was not retained following his brief stay at Bloomfield Road. Along with Luke Raisbeck (q.v.) he joined Carlisle United, and apart from a very brief spell with Chorley he remained with the Cumbrians for the remainder of his playing career. Highlights included promotion from the Lancashire Combination Division Two as champions in 1906-07, followed by a second place finish to Everton Reserve in 1907-08 and an appearance in the first round proper of the FA Cup for the first time in their history.
Appearances: FL: 2 apps 1 gl Total: 2 apps 1 gl

SCARR, John 'Jack' Geoffrey Stanley
Right half back
Born: Blackpool, 5th October 1874
Died: Fylde, July quarter 1961
Debut v Darwen (h) 16.4.97, won 1-0
CAREER: **Blackpool October 1896 to 1899.**

A reserve half back whose nine League appearances were spread over three seasons, Jack Scarr's four consecutive outings at the start of relegation season 1898-99 each ended in defeat, and he did not get another opportunity. In 1900 he was employed as a Stock and Share Broker, and later as a Land and Estate Agent.
Appearances: FL: 9 apps 0 gls Total: 9 apps 0 gls

SCOTT, John 'Jack' Arthur

Full back
5' 6½" 11st 3lbs
Born: Fleetwood, 25th September 1875
Died: Fleetwood, 7th September 1931
Debut v Glossop (a) 3.9.98, lost 1-4
CAREER: Fleetwood Swifts 1893. Fleetwood Rangers during season 1894-95, re-signed September 1897. **Blackpool May 1898 and re-signed November 1900**. Rossendale United August 1909. Fleetwood 1910.

Considered one of the best Blackpool players of his era, Jack Scott was reliable in any position on the field, but the position of full

back suited him best. As is usually the case with a local product, Scott became one of the most popular players associated with the club, and certainly no wearer of the teams' colours gave the club finer or more loyal service. While smaller than most full backs of the day, his speed off the mark served him well and his fitness enabled him to come through the most gruelling 90 minutes and still come out appearing "as fresh as a daisy", according to one observer. Quite remarkably between 1901 and 1907 he dominated the full back position, missing only two League matches and his overall appearance record was a fitting testiment to his fitness and consistency over a very long period. Captain of the side for five seasons, he left to join Rossendale United in August 1909, but after half a season he signed for Fleetwood and captained the side in the Lancashire Combination until the outbreak of war In his second season he led his team to success, winning the Lancashirre Junior Cup. Jack Scott died at his home, 85, Walmsley Street, Fleetwood, after a three-year illness at the age of 55.
Appearances: FL: 311 apps 16 gls FAC: 23 apps 1 gl Total: 334 apps 17 gls

SHARP, C. W.
Inside right 5' 6" 10st 8lbs
Born: Nottingham, *circa* 1891
Debut v Notts County (a) 24.9.13, lost 0-2
CAREER: Long Eaton St Helen's May 1909. Sutton Junction July 1911. **Blackpool May 1913.** Ilkeston United June 1914.

The 'Lancashire Daily Post Handbook 1913-14' announced Sharp's arrival at Blackpool as follows: "Inside-forward, who comes from Sutton Junction, for whom he scored 36 goals last season. Age 22, he is young, light and nimble." His departure was very much regretted by the Sutton Junction directors, who had been confident of retaining his services. The fact that the club had shown a loss of £160 in 1912-13, despite an excellent playing season, was no doubt a factor in the departure of their star man. Blackpool had the worst attack in the Football League in 1913-14, scoring just 33 goals in 38 League matches, with eleven of the total credited to Joe Lane, a reserve centre forward from Sunderland, who was signed in November 1913. Sharp had just three senior outings, and in each one the team failed to register a goal.
Appearances: FL: 3 apps 0 gls Total: 3 apps 0 gls

SHAW, George

Outside right
Born: Hollinwood, Oldham, 24th March 1890
Died: Blackpool, January quarter 1977
Debut v Barnsley (h) 18.12.09, drawn 0-0
CAREER: Blackpool amateur April 1909. Fleetwood amateur 1910. **Blackpool amateur March 1911.** Fleetwood amateur October 1911.

An injury sustained in a match against Everton Reserves was an unfortunate start for amateur wingman George Shaw who combined his football career with employment as a schoolmaster at Poulton. Described as "A very hard worker" by the Lancashire Daily Post annual of 1912-13, he was a regular at outside right for the Reserves, but made only infrequent appearances in the League side.
Appearances: FL: 6 apps 0 gls Total: 6 apps 0 gls

SIBBALD, John 'Jack' Patrick

Inside left
5' 8" 12st 0lbs
Born: Wallsend-on-Tyne, 12th September 1890
Died: Newcastle-on-Tyne, 20th August 1956
Debut v Leicester Fosse (h) 14.10.14, lost 1-2 (scored)
CAREER: Walker St Christopher 1907-08. Wallsend Elm Villa. Brentford March 1909. Wallsend Park Villa June 1913. **Blackpool June 1914**. Wallsend August 1920. West Stanley October 1920. **Blackpool again April 1921.** Southport July 1922. Walsall June 1924. Wallsend

August 1925 to 1928. Wallsend Park Villa Committee June 1929 and Secretary July 1930.

Jack Sibbald was working as a time clerk at a Wallsend Shipyard when offered a first opportunity of senior football by Brentford of the Southern League. He had returned north, however, before joining Blackpool for the last season of League football before the competition was abandoned for the duration of the Great War. After appearing regularly in 1919-20 he was allowed to leave to take up North-Eastern League football, many supporters being of the opinion that he should not have been allowed to depart. However, when he did return to Bloomfield Road for the 1921-22 season he was unable to lift a struggling side that finished in 19th place in Division Two, just two points better off than the two relegated clubs, Bradford Park Avenue and Bristol City. Two seasons with Southport, of the Third Division North, followed in which he scored 16 goals in 69 matches. A season with Walsall (12 goals in 38 matches) wound up his League career. He worked for twenty years as a clerical officer with the National Assistance Board up until September 1955, sadly dying after less than a year in retirement.
Appearances: FL: 70 apps 15 gls FAC: 3 apps 2 gls Total: 73 apps 17 gls

SPEIGHT, Thomas 'Tommy' Dean

Outside right
5' 8½" 10st 7lbs
Born: Heywood, 11th December 1878
Died: Hereford, 24th March 1958
Debut v New Brighton Tower (a) 1.9.1900, drawn 0-0
CAREER: South Shore Celtic 1896. South Shore Standard 1898. South Shore F.C. May 1898. **Blackpool May 1899, registered to play in FL matches July 1900.**

Outside right Tommy Speight started his football in 1896 with South Shore Celtic, for whom he played for two seasons. In the first season the Fylde League was started, the Celtic finished runners-up. The second season saw them win the South Shore Medal Competition. Leaving the Celtic he joined South Shore Standard of the Preston and District Amateur League, who won the championship and were also runners-up for the South Shore Medals, the Celtic beating them in the final. Speight's success as a forward had not gone unnoticed, and South Shore stepped in to sign him. After a season with them he joined Blackpool. He was a great success in season 1899-1900, contributing much in Blackpool's splendid display in the Lancashire Cup competition. (Blackpool reached the semi-final, losing after a replay, to Preston North End, who beat Burnley 1-0 in the final.) When Blackpool resumed in Division Two of the Football League in 1900-01, Tommy Speight was at outside right in the opening five matches, and despite the fact that his spell in the side resulted in three wins and two draws, he lost his place to the emerging Harold Hardman. A brother, Arthur (1873-1949) was a South Shore player. Tommy Speight was a joiner by trade.
Appearances: FL: 5 apps 0 gls Total: 5 apps 0 gls

SPENCER, Joseph 'Joe'
Left full back 5' 9" 11st 7lbs
Born: Newcastle-on-Tyne
Debut v Birmingham (h) 20.4.12, won 1-0
CAREER: Southport Park Villa. South Shields Parkside October 1909. **Blackpool May 1911**. Southend United September 1912. Southport Park Villa September 1912. Southend United April 1913.

There were few opportunities of first team football for Joe Spencer, with Crewdson and Gladwin Blackpool's recognised full back pairing. Following Gladwin's transfer to Sunderland, it was George Dale who took over his role at left full back, and it was not until the final month of the campaign that Joe Spencer made his two senior appearances. A move in the close season took him to Southend United, at that time operating in the Second Division of the Southern League. Thanks to an unbeaten home record, Southend won promotion to the First

Division, as runners-up to Cardiff City, who lost only one match throughout the season. In the FA Cup competition, Southend met Chelsea, of the First Division, at Stamford Bridge. They lost 5-2, with Bob Whittingham, the former Blackpool sharpshooter, on the mark with four goals, two from the penalty spot.
Appearances: FL: 2 apps 0 gls Total: 2 apps 0 gls

SPENCER, Stanley
Inside right
Born: Bury, 25th January 1881
Died: 1950
Debut v Manchester United (a) 9.4.04, lost 1-3 (scored)
CAREER: Bury Athenaeum. **Blackpool amateur May 1903.**

Stanley Spencer's Blackpool debut was memorable for the goal that he scored against Manchester United at Clayton. The 'Athletic News' reporting as follows: "Spencer's goal came from a shot from fully 40 yards range, and it sailed into the net with Harry Moger, United's goalkeeper, unable to get anywhere near to it". Sadly, however, Blackpool's chances of getting out of the last three in the table were further jeopardised by the 3-1 defeat, sustained in squally weather and on a heavy pitch, Blackpool's forwards being unable to make much headway against United's strong halves and backs. Stanley Spencer, who had deputised for the injured 'Geordie' Anderson, did not get another opportunity, but Blackpool did pull away from the lower reaches of the table, and clear of a re-election application, finishing in 15th place in the Division Two table.
Appearances: FL: 1 app 1 gl Total: 1 app 1 gl

STEVENSON, Charles Bertram

Inside right
Born: Grimethorpe, Sheffield, 26th May 1883
Died: Spilsby, Lincolnshire, July quarter 1966
Debut v Hull City (a) 17.10.08, lost 0-2
CAREER: Rotherham Town. Everton March 1908. **Blackpool June 1908**. Huddersfield Town August 1909. Mirfield United September 1910. Retford Town September 1913. Bird in Hand FC September 1914.

A native of Grimethorpe, near Sheffield, Stevenson was a lightweight forward who assisted a number of well-known clubs without graduating to senior level, his solitary outing for Blackpool being his only Football League appearance. This came in the wake of an injury list of no fewer than nine players, and this at the mid point of the second month of the season. As the local correspondent noted: "There were several alterations in the Blackpool squad, it is being reported that the team for the trip to Hull City will contained half-a-dozen 'second teamers.'" In the event, and with some re-shuffling of the pack, a fairly representative line up took to the field at Anlaby Road. A 2-0 defeat ensued in which the Blackpool forwards at times combined prettily, but failed to drive their attacks home. It was not a good weekend for the club, as the Reserves, with several new men in their team, went down by 4 goals to two to Bury Reserves at Bloomfield Road.
Appearances: FL: 1 app 0 gls Total: 1 app 0 gls

STIRLING, Robert Laidlaw
Outside right 5' 11" 13st 0lbs
Born: Kelvin, 26th February 1883
Died: Barrow-in-Furness, 26th January 1925
Debut v Leeds City (a) 30.1.09, lost 0-1
CAREER: Heart of Midlothian November 1906. Plymouth Argyle May 1907. **Blackpool August 1908**. Morton August 1909. Millwall Athletic September 1909

A wingman with the build of a full back, Robert Stirling's season with Blackpool was ruined by knee injuries. It was not until February that it was decided to try him in the League side, and this only after the state of the pitch was ascertained. In bright, frosty, weather at Leeds, the former Scottish junior international gave a sound exhibition, and the local correspondent suggested that his display was such as to give the utmost gratification to his directors. However, he was not given another opportunity and returned to Scotland to join Morton, most probably on trial, as he departed after just two appearances before journeying south to join Millwall Athletic, for whom he scored two goals in 15 Southern League matches. Some two years earlier, Stirling had assisted Plymouth Argyle to second place in the Southern League, scoring five goals in 16 League matches.
Appearances: FL: 2 apps 0 gls Total: 2 apps 0 gls

STIRZAKER, Henry 'Harry'/ 'Squash'
Centre half/Full back
Born: Fleetwood, July quarter 1869
Died: Fleetwood, 31st May 1938, age 68
Debut v Lincoln City (a) 5.9.96, lost 1-3
CAREER: Fleetwood Rangers. **Blackpool June 1896 and re-signed July 1900**. Lytham Institute September 1904.

Often referred too as 'Squash' Stirzaker, many years on his unusual nickname remains a mystery. A regular in Blackpool's defence for five seasons of League football, initially at full back and later, with great success, as centre half back. A typical match report summed up his virtues as follows: "Of the half backs, Stirzaker was the best, his lengthy frame always in the thick of the fray, and he never tired." He was particularly effective in 1900-01 when operating at times as a sixth forward from centre half, he netted seven goals in 35 matches. In the same season he was awarded a benefit, Liverpool providing the opposition. In 1911 he was employed as a fish packer with H. Hardy & Co, steam trawler owners. On Wednesday 21st January 1934, a benefit game was played for him. He was then in poor health, but must have derived consolation from the fact that, judging by the large attendance, he had not been forgotten. Fleetwood FC beat a Blackpool XI by the only goal of the game on the North Euston ground. In February 1945 the 'Fleetwood Chronicle' reported that: "A son of the former Blackpool footballer, the late Henry "Squash" Stirzaker, 33 years-old Lance Corporal Robert "Bob" Stirzaker is reported killed in action in Belgium. He was with the Royal Engineers & landed in France soon after D-Day."
Appearances: FL: 153 apps 13 gls FAC: 12 app 2 gls Total: 165 apps 15 gls

STUART, Alexander 'Alec'
Wing half back
Debut v Lincoln City (a) 5.9.96, lost 1-3
CAREER: South Shore May 1895. **Blackpool June 1896 to 1899.** Blackpool Electric FC February 1901.

In October 1899, the Blackpool and South Shore clubs could not reach an agreement over Alec Stuart's transfer. Five years earlier, Stuart had been playing for South Shore in the Lancashire League and when Blackpool were elected to Division Two of the Football League, Stuart "donned the blue & white", and played in 21 League matches in his first season. Problems arose when Blackpool failed to gain re-election to Division Two of the Football League at the close of the 1898-99 season, and returned to play in the Lancashire League. At this point South Shore demanded a transfer fee, presumably having retained his Lancashire League registration. As the local press stated at the time: "Blackpool are likely to be without Alec's services for some time yet." The outcome of the saga was not reported upon, but when Blackpool regained their League status in time to contest the 1900-01 season, Alec Stuart was not amongst the players signed.
Appearances: FL: 45 apps 1 gl FAC: 1 app 0 gls Total: 46 apps 1 gl

SWAN, Andrew 'Andy'
Centre/Inside forward 5' 9" 10st 11lbs
Born: Kinning Park, Glasgow, 28th December 1877
Died: Warragul, Victoria, SE Australia, 17th September 1964
Debut v Chelsea (h) 8.9.06, drawn 0-0
CAREER: Dalbeattie. Dalbeattie Star. Lincoln City November 1898. New Brompton May 1899. Barnsley May 1900. Woolwich Arsenal May 1901. Stockport County December 1901. St Mirren May 1902. Tottenham Hotspur May 1904. Partick Thistle May 1905. **Blackpool June 1906.** Workington July 1907. **Blackpool again August 1908.** Workington August 1909, re-signed March 1910.

Regarding this player's surname, only one of his many Football League clubs (Tottenham Hotspur) registered him as Andrew Swann. The others, including Blackpool, registered him as above. He began brightly in League football, scoring 10 goals in just 13 appearances for Lincoln City, and maintained an excellent scoring ratio until he reached Blackpool, but his career figures remained impressive – 35 goals in 89 League matches. In Scottish League football he scored eight goals in 33 appearances for St Mirren, and three in 16 matches for Partick Thistle. Andy Swan lived in Dalbeattie from the age of two to thirteen, and in Glasgow into the 1940s. After football he emigrated South East Australia. As a dairy farmer he worked in various locations including Budgeree, Johnstones Hill, Tooradin and Athlone. He served in the Galloway Volunteer Rifles and was later with the Gordon Highlanders until April 1919.
Appearances: FL: 26 apps 1 gl FAC: 1 app 0 gls Total: 27 apps 1 gl

SWARBRICK, Robert Lewis
Outside left 5' 7" 10st 7lbs
Born: St. Annes-on-Sea, October quarter 1881 (Baptised 11th December 1881)
Died: K.I.A. 2nd Battle of Passchendaele, 26th October 1917
Debut v Gainsborough Trinity (a) 21.11.1903, lost 1-3
CAREER: Bury Athenaeum. Oldham Athletic November 1901. **Blackpool February 1903.** Lytham 1904-05. Oldham Athletic again November 1905.

One of three brothers who all played in League football, and who were born to parents Robert Swarbrick and his wife Elizabeth (nee Lewis). Most notably, James was a Welsh Cup winner with Swansea Town in 1914, while George William played for Preston North End. Lewis' career was modest by comparison, two separate spells with Oldham Athletic in non-League days being quite undistinguished. After making just one senior appearance with Blackpool, a career change led him to emigrate to Canada, where he settled in Hamilton, West Ontario. He was employed in the cotton industry as a card room operative before returning to the UK in 1912. He enlisted as a Private in the 2/8th King's Liverpool (Irish Regiment) but sadly lost his life in 1917, official sources stated that his father was sent his dead son's effects, amounting to £19. 6 shillings and 9 pence.
Appearances: FL: 1 app 0 gls Total: 1 app 0 gls

TAYLOR, Thomas
Inside right
Born: Probably at Bolton
Debut v Barnsley (h) 20.3.1901, drawn 1-1
CAREER: **Blackpool May 1900.**

Taylor had a lengthy wait for his League debut, which finally came when injuries to Burden, Evans and Anderson resulted in five changes, two positional, for the visit of Barnsley. In bitterly cold weather and before about 500 spectators, Taylor wasted two opportunities to score – "A wretched attempt at scoring" and shortly afterwards "Taylor broke through, and with only the goalkeeper to beat, shot wide." Blackpool were a goal behind at the interval, but equalised with only minutes to spare, Birket heading home from a fine centre from amateur international wingman, Harold Hardman. Blackpool scored only 33 goals in 34 League matches in 1900-01, the worst scoring record in the two Divisions of the League, but they finished in twelfth position in Division Two, well clear of the foot of the table.
Appearances: FL: 1 app 0 gls Total: 1 app 0 gls

THOMPSON, Fred
Centre half back
Debut v Small Heath (h) 23.1.97, lost 1-3
CAREER: South Shore. **Blackpool August 1895, registered for FL matches July 1896**. Stalybridge Rovers May 1897, and re-signed August 1901.

All but one of Fred Thompson's senior appearances came in the final month of the 1896-97 season when he took over the role of Harry Stirzaker at centre half back. Two losses, two wins and a draw resulted, with five goals scored and five conceded. It was Blackpool's first season in the Football League and they finished eighth in the table. In the period to 1914-15, they only once finished higher, being seventh in 1910-11, thanks to 18 goals in 32 League matches from Joe Clennell, who was snapped up by Blackburn Rovers in the final month of the season.
Appearances: FL: 6 apps 0 gls Total: 6 apps 0 gls

THOMPSON, Fred "Freddie" (No 2)
Goalkeeper
Debut v Glossop (a) 27.3.15, won 3-1
CAREER: Hamilton United (Ontario, Canada). Fleetwood July 1914. **Blackpool March 1915.**

In the final League season before World War One caused the suspension of normal League fare, the Blackpool club found themselves short of cover in the goalkeeping department. This came about following the transfer of regular custodian, Jimmy Kidd, to Bolton Wanderers in March 1915. Initially, Blackpool turned locally to sign Freddie Thompson, who was guarding Fleetwood's goal, and over the Easter period he did an excellent job, two home wins against Huddersfield Town and Stockport County following on from his debut in the away win against Glossop. Freddie Thompson had, a year earlier, returned from Canada where he had been keeping goal for Hamilton United, of Ontario,
Appearances: FL: 3 apps 0 gls Total: 3 apps 0 gls

THORPE, Levi 'Levy'

Wing half back
5' 7" 10st 7lbs
Born: Seaham Harbour, 18th November 1889
Died: Blackpool, 26th February 1935
Debut v Leicester Fosse (h) 29.3.11, won 2-0
CAREER: Seaham Albion. Seaham Harbour August 1908. Seaham White Star May 1909. Seaham Harbour June 1910. **Blackpool February 1911**. Burnley October 1913. (Wartime guest player with Leeds City, Bradford PA, Blackpool and Manchester City). Blackburn Rovers February 1920, fee £3,000 Lincoln City September 1922. Rochdale June 1924 to cs 1926. Farnworth Town.

Levi Thorpe Joined Blackpool from Seaham Harbour towards the close of the 1910-11 season. From his first associations with the club he showed consistently good form at left half-back, his stylish and effective play being greatly admired. Quick on the ball, excellent in headwork and an able purveyor of the defence splitting pass to his forwards, he was additionally a gentleman both on the field and off it. Two successive ever-present seasons attracted interest from Bradford City in early October 1913, and although the directors of the Blackpool and Bradford City clubs had come to terms for the players' transfer, the player refused the offer, in spite of better renumeration and improved prospects. Later in the same month, however, Levi Thorpe was transferred to Burnley, assisting them at either side of the Great War, during which time he initially worked in munitions and found time to assist a number of clubs as a guest player. He later served in the 1/4th North Lancashire Regiment, and was wounded. In the first postwar season he was transferred from Burnley to Blackburn Rovers. He gave excellent value to all of his five League clubs, his career aggregate total being 349 matches and 14 goals. Sadly, he suffered from a lengthy illness before dying at just 35 years of age, shortly after Blackpool had played in a benefit game for him.

Appearances: FL: 92 apps 1 gl FAC: 6 apps 0 gls Total: 98 apps 1 gl
Honours: FL representative v Irish League, 21st October 1921.

THRELFALL, Edward 'Threlly'

Right half back
Born: Kirkham, 6th January 1880
Died: Wesham, near Kirkham, 19th December 1941
Debut v New Brighton Tower (a) 1.9.00, drawn 0-0
CAREER: Kirkham F.C. Wesham F.C. 1898. South Shore June 1898. **Blackpool July 1900 to1911.** Kirkham & Wesham September 1912.

A Blackpool stalwart for eleven seasons of League football, Edward Threlfall was also a noted pedestrian and track athlete, quarter mile races being his speciality. Popularly know as "Threlly" he was always the most consistent player, being a glutton for work, playing the game from the first to the final whistle. From right half back he was a real aid to his forwards and an effective stumbling block to the opposition. In March 1906, Bolton Wanderers provided the opposition in his well-deserved benefit match. It was reported, during his final season, that he had taken up farming at the Wesham House Farm, Kirkham.
Appearances: FL: 317 apps 11 gls FAC: 24 apps 2 gls Total: 341 apps 13 gls

TILLOTSON, Stephen 'Steve'

Goalkeeper
5' 10" 13st 0lbs
Born: Brierfield, 18th April 1884
Died: Skipton, 7th September 1961
Debut v Stockport County (a) 2.9.07, drawn 1-1
CAREER: Wandering Boys F.C. (Nelson). Nelson F.C. 1901. Burnley amateur August 1903. Brierfield Swifts. Colne A.F.C. April 1904. **Blackpool May 1907**. Burnley August 1909 to October 1911. (Burnley wartime guest season 1917-18).

Born at Nelson on 18th April 1884, Steve Tillotson learnt his football on the Nelson Recreation ground with a team known as the Wandering Boys. He was working as a cotton spinner when he joined Nelson in 1901, later with Burnley on amateur forms in August 1903, and joined Colne, in April 1904, from Brierfield Swifts, members of the Burnley and District Amateur League. With this team he was remarkably successful, winning the championship of the League, the North-East Lancashire Shield, and they also finished runners-up in the North-East Lancashire Challenge Cup. Described as: "A well-built and athletic looking youth," he became a great favourite at Colne, guarding the breach with skill and daring for three seasons. In the championship season, 1905-06, he received several words of praise for his extraordinary exhibition in the Junior Cup Final against Atherton Church House at Deepdale. Seeming to know by instinct exactly what to do, he did it with the greatest neatness and accuracy. At times his goal was in the greatest danger, but he defied all-comers enabling his team to lift the trophy by one goal to nil. Colne's stay in the First Division was of short duration, not helped by an injury to Tillotson in the opening match of the new season, a 0-2 defeat at Oldham Athletic, which sidelined him for six matches. His understudies proved to be poor substitutes, and the team never recovered from their indifferent start. Despite the relegation, Tillotson had guarded his goal in a fashion that gained him a wide reputation, many clubs seeking his services towards the close of the season. Blackpool won the race for his signature in May 1907. In two seasons at Bloomfield Road, Tillotson appeared in the first 17 League matches of season 1907-08 before being succeeded by Bill Fiske, and spending all but one match in reserve in the following season. Transferred to Burnley in August 1909, he made his debut in a 4-2 win against Wolverhampton Wanderers at Turf Moor on 13th November 1909. As understudy to Clarets' legendary Jerry Dawson, whose career spanned 21 years and 568 appearances, Tillotson played in only

eight first team matches, but remained a regular in the Clarets' Reserve eleven until October 1911. During the First World War period, he returned to Turf Moor to assist his former team in eight matches during season 1917-18. Employed as a foreman in a weaving shed, and a resident in Skipton for most of his days, Steve Tillotson died there on 7th September 1961, aged 77.
Appearances: FL: 19 apps 0 gls Total: 19 apps 0 gls

TONGE, Benjamin 'Ben'
Inside right 5' 8" 10st 4lbs
Born: Openshaw, 8th February 1883
Died: Thornton Cleveleys, 11th March 1972
Debut v Clapton Orient (h) 23.1.09, lost 1-3
CAREER: Altrincham. Oldham Athletic November 1904. Altrincham cs 1905. Denton September 1905. Atherton May 1906. **Blackpool January 1909**. Darwen September 1909. Stalybridge FC September 1911. Grantham August 1912.

To fill the vacancy caused by the transfer of Bob Whittingham to Bradford City, Blackpool signed Ben Tonge, a lightly built inside forward, from the Atherton club. It was rather optimistic of the Blackpool committee to expect a player without previous League experience to provide a ready-made replacement for their departed star forward, and perhaps predictably, after three matches, all of which ended in defeat, Ben Tonge was dropped, being recalled at outside right for a final outing against West Bromwich Albion on 3rd April, a match which was lost 1-5. Ben's younger brother, Charlie, an outside left, was also a player with Oldham Athletic in season 1904-05. His final outing for the Latics was his most memorable as he was in the side that thrashed Newton-le-Willows 11-0 on 7th January 1905. Only two of the Latics forwards scored in the match – Shoreman scoring six goals and Plumpton five.
Appearances: FL: 4 apps 0 gls Total: 4 apps 0 gls

TOPPING, Robert William
Outside-left
Born: Blackpool, 4th June 1886
Died: Blackpool, 2nd April 1984
Debut v Leicester Fosse (h) 17.3.06, lost 0-1
CAREER: **Blackpool amateur March 1906**. Kirkham March 1907. Fleetwood. Blackpool Athletic. Fleetwood.

Local amateur wingman Robert Topping appeared in seven of the final matches of season 1905-06, replacing another amateur wingman John Hollingworth. A successful trial in the Reserves against Haslingden had earned him the promotion, the Lancashire Evening Post's report of the match included the following: "Blackpool introduced Topping, a local youth, who proved pretty "nippy" at getting round an opponent."
Appearances: FL: 7 apps 0 gls Total: 7 apps 0 gls

TULLOCH, Albert 'Bert'

Full back
5' 7½" 11st 0lbs
Born: North Shields, 23rd February 1889
Died: Marton, Blackpool, 15th February 1953
Debut v Leicester Fosse (h) 24.10.14, lost 1-2
CAREER: Scotswood. Wingate Albion. **Blackpool May 1913**. (Wartime guest player with Scotswood and Ashington) **Appointed Blackpool trainer May 1924; masseur June 1927; head trainer July 1927.** Nelson trainer July 1928 to November **1930.**

At either right or left full back Bert Tulloch was considered one of the cleverest defenders in the Second Division, both in tackling and distribution. After a steady start to his Blackpool career – a season in reserve before breaking into the League side in season 1914-15 – he blossomed after the Great War, being rarely absent in the first three seasons of post war football, in which Blackpool finished fourth in Division Two in successive seasons. His long service with the club continued as trainer and masseur after his playing career ended.
Appearances: FL: 188 apps 0 gls FAC: 8 apps 0 gls Total: 196 apps 0 gls

TURLEY, Harry

Inside right
5' 8" 12st 8lbs
Born: Snedshill, Telford, Salop, 4th January 1891
Died: Oakengates, 16th November1971
Debut v Hull City (h) 6.9.13, drawn 2-2
CAREER: Wellington St George's. St George's Victoria October 1909. Wolverhampton Wanderers February 1911. Stafford Rangers July 1912. **Blackpool June 1913.** Stafford Rangers September 1919. Wellington St. George July 1920.

Of Harry Turley's seven first team appearances in 1913-14, three were made in the opening fixtures, and three in the final matches of the season. His late inclusion coming in the wake of Tommy Charlton's very serious head injury in the match against Leicester Fosse on 10th April. Turley scored his only League goal in the penultimate fixture, a 2-2 home draw against Stockport County. Said to have played well in the Reserves, he was retained for a further season, but added only another four League outing to his total. Considering the fact that he had scored 31 goals for Stafford Rangers in 1912-13, his senior career was disappointing, as he had also failed to reach first team level with Wolverhampton Wanderers.
Appearances: FL: 11 apps 1 gl Total: 11 apps 1 gl

WADDINGTON, John

Outside left
5' 8½" 12st 0lbs
Born: Manchester, 21st April 1879
Died: Blackpool, October quarter 1954
Debut v Gainsborough Trinity (h) 22.10.04, drawn 2-2
CAREER: Poulton. Chorley September 1901. Liverpool April 1902. Poulton April 1903. Glentoran 1903. **Blackpool May 1904.** Southport Central June 1905. Chorley September 1906. **Blackpool May 1907.** Blackpool Athletic November 1908. Haslingden November 1909.

A very successful season with Glentoran, after being with Poulton, Chorley, and Liverpool, saw the pacy wingman selected by the Irish League against the Football League at Valley Parade, Bradford in October 1903. The Football League won 2-1, Waddington scoring the Irish League's goal. Despite an excellent first season with Blackpool – eight goals in 38 matches - John Waddington, along with Alf Jolly, was allowed to move on to Southport Central for their first season on their present ground, known as Ash Lane at that time. Waddington led the Central's scoring list with eleven in 40 matches and moved on to Chorley for whom he scored 39 goals in 1906-07. One observer noting that this was more than the whole of the Blackpool team had scored in the same season! What was not mentioned, however, was the fact that his goals were scored against Lancashire Combination Division Two defences, and on his return to Blackpool for a second spell, he failed to score in nine League matches. John Waddington served as a Corporal Gunner with the RGA in World War One.
Appearances: FL: 32 apps 6 gls FAC: 6 apps 2 gls Total: 38 apps 8 gls
Honours: Irish League representative, 1 app.v Football League

WAKE, Bertram 'Bert'
Centre forward 6' 1"
Born: Wincanton, 13th February 1885
Died: South Barrow, Somerset, 30th March 1955
Debut v Chelsea (h) 8.9.06, drawn 0-0
CAREER: Salisbury City August 1905. **Blackpool amateur May, professional September 1906.** Wolverhampton Wanderers July 1907. Salisbury City September 1907. Southampton September 1909. Salisbury City December 1909. Bitterne Guild October 1911.

Bert Wake joined Blackpool after showing promise as a centre forward with Salisbury City of the Western League. Standing a little over six feet in height and with a build to match, he showed enough in training to win a professional contract but in the event he was

just one of six different centre forwards fielded, the best of which, William Grundy, headed the scoring list with just eight goals. Bert Wakes' penultimate appearance came in a 1-2 defeat against Wolverhampton Wanderers, and he must have impressed the Wanderers' committee as he moved to Molineux in the close season. With a loan spell with his old club Salisbury City inbetween, he made just four League appearances for the Wolves, his one goal coming in a 2-1 defeat at Fulham. A short spell with Southampton did not include a first team appearance.
Appearances: FL: 4 apps 0 gls Total: 4 apps 0 gls

WALKER, Thomas August

nside-left
5' 8" 12st 8lbs
Born: Seaton Delaval, October quarter 1882
Debut v Hull City (a) 17.10.08, lost 0-2
CAREER: Thornley. Sunderland June 1903. Seaton Delaval October 1904. Sunderland May 1905. West Stanley September 1906. Fulham May 1907. Watford January 1908. **Blackpool August 1908.** Seaton Delaval January 1910. West Stanley May 1910. New Hartley Rovers October 1910. Seaton Delaval November 1912.

Without a senior appearance for either Sunderland or Fulham, a mid term move to Watford finally brought Thomas Walker first team football. At either centre forward or inside right he netted five goals in 15 Southern League matches. In the summer he joined Blackpool and three goals in eight appearances suggested that he might have been worth more opportunities in a season when Blackpool were obliged, for financial reasons, to transfer their best forward, Bob Whittingham, who had scored 13 goals in 22 matches at the point of his departure to Bradford City.
Appearances: FL: 8 apps 3 gls Total: 8 apps 3 gls

WALLACE, William
Left half back
Debut v Luton Town (a) 25.3.99, lost 2-3
CAREER: Blackpool March 1899.

William Wallace made his solitary senior appearance on a bitterly cold afternoon at Luton, with driving snow and rain, conditions that resulted in an estimated attendance of "not more than 800". Blackpool were short of four regular first team men in Stuart, Atherton, Parr and Williams, and in the circumstances were unfortunate not to take a point. The 2-3 defeat replicating the score in the earlier meeting with the Hatters at the Athletic Ground on 26th November. The 'Luton News' considered that Fletcher, Blackpool's goalkeeper, was their best man, with Parkinson and Birket also noticeable.
Appearances: FL: 1 app 0 gls Total: 1 app 0 gls

WALTERS, Charles Edwin
Centre half back 5' 8" 10st 8lbs
Born: Leek, 25th June 1889
Died: Hemsworth, West Riding, October quarter 1959
Debut v Lincoln City (h) 12.11.10, won 5-1
CAREER: Chesterton White Star November 1909. **Blackpool June 1910.** Macclesfield October 1912. Goole Town September 1913.

Signed as cover for the centre half position, Walters made his debut in the season's best win against Lincoln City in which another recruit from Staffordshire, centre forward Fred Morley, netted a hat trick. With Jimmy Connor continuing to dominate the centre half berth, Walters was restricted to just six first team outings. He was transfer listed with a fee of £25 fixed by the Football League Committee in September 1912, but he did not find another League club. In 1911 he was employed as a silk warehouseman and later worked as a collier before enlisting in the Royal Engineers, working in special signal training. He was discharged in November 1918.
Appearances: FL: 6 apps 0 gls Total: 6 apps 0 gls

WATSON, Lionel Thompson

Inside-forward
Born: Southport, 27th May 1882
Died: Blackpool, October quarter 1945
Debut v Grimsby Town (a) 19.12.08, lost 1-2
CAREER: All Saints' School (Southport). Laurel Rovers (Southport). High Park (Southport) 1899. Southport Central 1900. Manchester City July 1901. Blackburn Rovers October 1902. West Ham United May 1905. **Blackpool December 1908.**

Lionel Watson was restricted to just a single League appearance for Manchester City, but after a slow start with Blackburn Rovers he was fully established by season 1903-04, leading the scoring list with 14 League goals. After appearing in 61 League and Cup matches and scoring 20 goals he was transferred to West Ham United of the Southern League for whom he scored 27 goals in 80 League and Cup matches. 1906-07 was his best season, his 12 goals in 32 League matches included hat tricks against Luton Town and Fulham. Recruited by Blackpool in mid season 1908-09, he was unable to establish a place in a poor side that finished at the foot of Division Two. Outside of the game he worked as an Auctioneer and for a spell from 1916 he emigrated to Canada to work in farming.
Appearances: FL: 1 app 0 gls Total: 1 app 0 gls

WESTON, William

Centre or Inside forward
5' 9" 11st 6lbs
Born: Southwick, County Durham, 5th September 1882
Died: Sunderland, January quarter 1948
Debut v Derby County (a) 30.11.07, lost 1-2
CAREER: Southwick May 1904, & re-signed May 1905. Sunderland amateur 1905. Crystal Palace May 1906. Burslem Port Vale 1907. **Blackpool July 1907**. Heywood United July 1908. Nelson August 1909. Spennymoor United February 1910. Houghton Rovers January 1911. Southwick September 1911.

William Weston commenced in senior football with Crystal Palace but featured little in first team matches in a season that featured an FA Cup adventure that quite shook the football world with wins against Rotherham County, Newcastle United (away), Fulham and Brentford before elimination in the hands of Everton, after a replay. After the briefest of associations with Burslem Port Vale, Weston arrived at Blackpool and appeared in 27 League and Cup matches in his first season, scoring five goals. He left at the conclusion of the following season in which Blackpool finished at the foot of Division Two, despite a bright opening when Weston scored in each of his first two matches, A 1-0 home win against Oldham Athletic, and a 1-1 draw at Clapton Orient. Two seasons of Lancashire Combination football prceded his return to native parts, initially with Spennymoor United. Born of Scottish parents, for decades he was employed as a shipyard caulker, and by 1939 was working as boilermaker's caulker and living in Southwick.
Appearances: FL: 45 apps 9 gls FAC: 2 apps 1 gl Total: 47 apps 10 gls

WHALLEY, Arthur

Half back
5' 8" 11st 10lbs
Born: Openshaw, 5th December 1887
Died: Wythenshawe, 23 November 1952
CAREER: Wigan Town. Brynn Central. **Blackpool March 1908**. Manchester United June 1909, fee £50. (Wartime guest player with Clapton Orient and Queens Park Rangers.) Southend United September 1920. Charlton Athletic August 1921. Millwall

October 1924. Barrow trainer-coach December 1926.
Debut v Chesterfield (a) 7.11.08, lost 1-3

Arthur Whalley's birth was registered as Arthur Boot, and in 1911 he was still known by this surname. He lived with his unmarried uncle, John Whalley, whose surname he took. One opinion regarding Arthur Whalley when with Blackpool at the outset of his career ran as follows: "Whalley is trimly built and a neat and quick player relying entirely on skill and purity of method. He seems always to be in the right place, and is clever with his headwork, intervenes aptly, and uses the ball to best advantage. With such a recommendation it was perhaps unsurprising that he was quickly spotted by bigger clubs, and it was Manchester United who secured his signature for a fee of £50 and the promise of the proceeds of a match between United and Blackpool.
Arthur Whalley was with Manchester United when they moved from Clayton to their present home at Old Trafford in February 1910. At either side of World War One – during which he served as a sergeant in the Middlesex Regiment – he recorded 106 League and Cup appearances and scored six goals for United, winning a League championship medal in 1911. A broad-shouldered, well built half- back he gave excellent service to all of his clubs and came close to international class but was unfortunate to be seriously injured in the North versus South international trial at Roker Park in January 1914. Appointed trainer-coach to Barrow in December 1926, his single playing appearance was made in an emergency, and was the only occasion that Barrow fielded a forty year-old centre forward! Arthur Whalley represented the Football League against the Irish League in October 1913. When he retired from the game he became a bookmaker in Manchester.
Appearances: FL: 6 apps 2 gls FAC: 1 app 1 gls Total: 7 apps 3 gls
Honours: FL representative, 1 app 1913 (Manchester United) FL Division 1 champions 1911

WHITESIDE, Edward 'Eddie'

Inside right
5' 7" 11st 0lbs
Born: Lytham, 28th June 1886
Died: Fleetwood, 28th February 1963
Debut v Wolverhampton Wanderers (a) 5.9.08, drawn 2-2
CAREER: Brynn Central. **Blackpool May 1908**. Rossendale United October 1909. Norwich City May 1910. New Brompton July 1911. Rossendale United September 1912.

Auburn-haired Eddie Whiteside appeared in six consecutive matches, replacing Bertie Lyon at centre forward after the opening day draw with Barnsley. Considering the fact that only one defeat occurred during his run in the side, Whiteside was probably worth more opportunities in a season when the team's form nosedived into a re-election application, finishing at the foot of Division Two. After a spell with Rossendale United, Whiteside joined Norwich City of the Southern League. In addition to his seven goals in 38 League and Cup matches, he netted two hat tricks for the Reserves, in what must have been entertaining matches against Cromer (won 11-6) and Luton Town (7-2). A season with New Brompton (forerunners of Gillingham) was only noticeable by the director's threat to wind up the club if attendances did not improve substantially. A second spell with Rossendale United wound up his playing career.
Appearances: FL: 6 apps 0 gls Total: 6 apps 0 gls

WHITTINGHAM, Robert 'Bob'

Inside forward
5' 8" 11st 12lbs
Born: Goldenhill, Tunstall, December 1888
Died: Goldenhill, Tunstall, 9th June 1926
Debut v Stockport County (a) 1.9.07, drawn 1-1 (scored)
CAREER: Goldenhill Villa amateur. Goldenhill Wanderers

amateur. Stoke amateur May 1902. Crewe Alexandra May 1906. **Blackpool July 1907**. Bradford City January 1909. Chelsea April 1910, fee £1,300. South Shields May 1914. (Wartime guest player with Chelsea, Port Vale, Nelson, Crompton's and Stoke.) Stoke, permanently September 1919. Stoke United December 1920. Macclesfield February 1921. Scunthorpe & Lindsay United June 1921. Wrexham November 1922. Goldenhill Wanderers December 1923.

A strong, well built young player, Bob Whittingham earned the reputation of being one of the best goal scorers in Division Two. In his first season he headed Blackpool's scoring list with 15 goals in 32 appearances, and in the following season, prior to his transfer to Bradford City, he had been responsible for nearly half of the goals scored by the team. When approached by Bradford City for Whittingham's transfer, a fee of £1,000 was quoted, but after negotiations lasting practically all day, Blackpool's directors agreed to accept a sum of £800. It was after midnight when the player signed the necessary papers for his transfer. The sum received enabled the Blackpool club to pay off its liabilities, amounting to £500 at the time. The improvement in the Bradford City attack was immediately apparent, Whittingham receiving many of his best openings from the accurate centres of Harold Hardman (q.v.) the former Blackpool wingman. After scoring 31 goals in 45 League matches, Whittingham was transferred to Chelsea, who were hoping that his goals would take them to promotion to Division One, this was achieved in 1911-12 when they finished as runners-up, on goal average, to Derby County. He departed Chelsea with an outstanding record, having netted 80 goals in 129 appearances. Transferred to Stoke in September 1919 he scored eight goals in 18 League matches, taking his career figures to 138 goals in 236 League matches for his four League clubs. He was working as a bus conductor at the time of his early death from pulmonary tuberculosis. Bob was a younger brother of Sam Whittingham (q.v.)
Appearances: FL: 54 apps 28 gls Total: 58 apps 28 gls

Honours: FL representative v Scottish League (scored two goals) 1919. England "Victory" International v Scotland in 1919.

WHITTINGHAM, Samuel 'Sam' Littleton

Half back/Full back
5' 7½" 10st 8lbs
Born: Sandyford, 24th February 1882
Died: Upper Agbrigg, West Riding, July quarter 1958
Debut v Barnsley (h) 2.9.09, drawn 1-1
CAREER: Goldenhill Wanderers. Stoke May 1902. Burslem Port Vale August 1903. Crewe Alexandra May 1906. **Blackpool May 1908**. Huddersfield Town May 1910 Mirfield United. Rossendale United July 1911. Morley FC February 1912. Mirfield United September 1913.

The elder brother of Bob Whittingham (q.v.) Sam assisted Goldenhill Wanderers and Stoke, followed by a three-year stay with Burslem Port Vale. A regular in the side for two of the three seasons, he totalled 71 League and Cup matches, scoring three goals. Two seasons with Crewe Alexandra of the Birmingham & District League followed. Crewe were winners of the Cheshire Senior Cup in April 1907 and were runners up in the League in the following season, four points behind the champions, Aston Villa Reserves. In May 1908 Sam Whittingham was reunited with his brother Bob at Blackpool. Sam was accompanied by full back Jonathan Poulson. He, however, was back and playing for Crewe in October, presumably having been signed on trial. Sam, meanwhile, settled in immediately at left full back, eventually taking over the role that had been so consistently filled by Jack Scott, prior to his retirement. Transferred to Huddersfield Town in 1910, Sam failed to reach League level at Leeds Road.
Appearances: FL: 48 apps 0 gls FAC: 3 apps 0 gls Total: 51 apps 0 gls

WHITTLE, Harry
Centre forward
Debut v Barnsley (a) 9.1.04, drawn 2-2
CAREER: All Saints FC. **Blackpool amateur November 1903.**

For their trip to Barnsley, Blackpool were handicapped in the matter of injured players. John Carthy, who had not recovered from a knock that he sustained in the previous match, was replaced in the team by amateur centre forward Harry Whittle. Described as: "A fine strapping youth" Whittle was said to be somewhat nervous on his debut, but overall made a favourable impression. He was selected for the following week's encounter with Lincoln City, but was on holiday at the time, and didn't return in time to appear! In the following month he appeared against Burton United, on a very heavy Bloomfield Road pitch. Two rather unkind match reports stated that all of the forwards, with the exception of Whittle, were successful. (Blackpool won 4-1). Another scribe reported: "There were great hopes of Whittle doing well at centre forward, but he was of little use after the first few minutes of the game. This position is one that will have to be attended to."
Appearances: FL: 2 apps 0 gls Total: 2 apps 0 gls

WILCOX, Thomas 'Tom' Walter James
Goalkeeper 5' 10" 11st 8lbs
Born: On international waters in 1879 (Birth registered at St. Stephen's, Stepney, on 9th January 1881, on return from America)
Died: Blackpool, 10th October 1963
Debut v Barnsley (a) 1.9.06, lost 2-3
CAREER: Millwall Athletic Reserves. Cray Wanderers September 1904. Woolwich Arsenal Reserves. Coventry City October 1905. **Blackpool May 1906.** Manchester United August 1907. Carlisle United July 1909. Huddersfield Town January 1911. Goole Town August 1912. Abergavenny F.C.

The son of a sea captain, Tom Wilcox was born at sea on board the four-masted barque 'Grassendale', under sail and bound for America. From the age of seventeen he lived in America, and it was in the States that his sporting prowess first became evident when he won the World Punchball Championship. A sport with pugilistic overtones; it was more in the nature of a gymnastic routine, centred around a punch ball, supported on a spring shaft. Moving back to England at about the turn of the century, Wilcox successfully took up goalkeeping. He assisted many prominent clubs in the South of England before moving to Blackpool to replace the popular Arthur Hull, who had departed after five seasons of excellent service. Wilcox proved to be a worthy successor, missing only one first team match in his single season at Bloomfield Road, being undefeated in thirteen of his 38 appearances. A move to Manchester United proved less rewarding, as he was one of four goalkeepers on United's books, with Harry Moger the regular first-team custodian. Wilcox did, however, play twice in League matches in 1907-08, and was awarded a gold medal by the club, to commemorate their first League championship. While living in Manchester he also worked as area manger for the Zonophone Gramophone Company.After leaving United he assisted Carlisle United to win the Cumbrian Cup. At the outbreak of war he volunteered and served with The Royal Welsh Fusiliers. After demob he had two tobacconist's shops in Preston, which he sold in 1938 and lived in retirement at Blackpool, where he died at the age of 83 years in 1962.
Note: The 9ct gold medal, awarded to Tom Wilcox by Manchester United, was sold at auction on 14th October 1992. It realised £1,500 at the hammer.
Appearances: FL: 37 apps 0 gls FAC: 1 app 0 gls Total: 38 apps 0 gls

WILKINSON, Fred 'Sonny'

Inside left
5' 10½" 12st 0lbs
Born: Bury, 22nd February 1889
Died: Norton, Stockton-on-Tees, 31st December 1965
Debut v Grimsby Town (a) 3.9.12, drawn 1-1
CAREER: St Augustine's. Lancaster F.C. October 1908. Norwich City May

1910. Darlington (trial) July, permanent December 1911. **Blackpool August 1912.** Stalybridge Celtic May 1913. Newport County September 1913. Stalybridge Celtic May 1914. Watford August 1919, fee £50. Stoke June 1921. Bury St Edmonds. Hurst October 1922 to January 1924.

Signed from Darlington along with Tom Heslop (q.v.), Fred Wilkinson showed early promise as a 17 year-old half back with Lancaster F.C. of the Second Division of the Lancashire Combination. Moving on to Norwich City he appeared in 66 Southern League matches, scoring five goals, being ever-present in season 1910-11. Blackpool finished at the bottom of Division Two in Wilkinson's season at Bloomfield Road in which he vied with Wilf Gillow for the inside left berth. He would doubtless have enjoyed scoring the winning goal against his hometown club, Bury, on 14th September but he failed register another. After the Great War he spent two seasons with Watford, of the Southern League, but made just three appearances for Stoke before a knee injury ended his senior career.
Appearances: FL: 15 apps 1 gl Total: 15 apps 1 gl

WILLIAMS, Frank
Centre half back
Debut v Loughborough (h) 8.10.98, won 2-1
CAREER: South Shore. Blackpool Grammar School. **Blackpool September 1898 and re-signed June 1900.**

One of two amateur half backs to assist Blackpool who were assistant schoolmasters at Blackpool Grammar School, Frank Williams settled immediately into the first team at centre half back, missing only three matches following an impressive debut in a 2-1 win against Loughborough. The other scholastic recruit, Oswald D. Parker, did not appear in the League side. Blackpool lost their League status following an unsuccessful application for re-election, but they were back after just one season away. Frank Williams re-signed but did not get another senior outing, Harry Stirzaker making just one short of maximum appearances at centre half during the season.

Appearances: FL: 27 apps 1 gl FAC: 2 apps 0 gls Total: 29 apps 1 gl

WILSON, Frank
Right half back
Born: Stockton, January quarter 1875
Died: 1898
Debut v Burnley (a) 4.9.97, lost 1-5
CAREER: Bishop Auckland. Gravesend F.C. Aston Villa 1896. Tottenham Hotspur. **Blackpool June 1897.** Aston Villa cs 1898.

In June 1898 the 'Ross Gazette' reported on an inquest that was held at Sedgfield regarding the death of Frank Wilson (age 23) a professional footballer: "Wilson, after playing in the Amateur Cup Final for Bishop Auckland, was signed by Gravesend as a professional. Later he played for Tottenham Hotspur, and last season for Blackpool. He was signed by Aston Villa for the coming season, but was committed to an asylum. The cause of death was given as maniacal exhaustion. About a year ago, a Portsmouth doctor advised deceased to give up footballing. The verdict was in accordance with the medical testimony." Despite the fact that Wilson had been advised to retire from playing during his season with Blackpool, there had been no outward signs of the impending disaster, as he had been one of Blackpool's best players, being particularly impressive when handed a settled role at right half back in mid season.
Appearances: FL: 25 apps 1 gl FAC: 1 app 0 gls Total: 26 apps 1 gl
Honours: (Bishop Auckland) FA Amateur Cup winner v Royal Artillery (Portsmouth) at Leicester 28th March 1896.

WILSON, George

Centre-half
5' 10" 11st 0lbs
Born: Kirkham, Blackpool, 14 January 1892
Died: Blackpool, 25 November 1961
Debut v Leeds City (a) 17.2.12, lost 0-1
CAREER: Sacred Heart School. Preston Schoolboys. Catholic College

(Preston). Willows Rovers. Stanley Villa. Fleetwood amateur. Willows Rovers. Morecambe 1911. **Blackpool amateur December 1911, professional January 1912**. Sheffield Wednesday March 1920, fee £3,000. Nelson July 1925, fee £2,000, a then record fee paid by a Third Division club. Retired July 1930.

George Wilson began in junior football as a forward, and eventually found his way to Blackpool after playing in just five games at centre forward for Morecambe. A faltering start in Blackpool's Reserves took an upturn when he scored his first goal against Manchester United Reserves at Bloomfield Road, and, on the evening of the match, he signed his first professional contract. He made his League debut in the following month at Leeds City. In a 1922 interview, Wilson admitted that his career was going nowhere until Blackpool's assistant trainer George Anderson, a one time famous centre-half of Blackburn Rovers, suggested to the directors of the club that Wilson would make an ideal centre half. Despite a 5 – 0 thrashing at Derby County in his first outing in the new position Wilson maintained his place until the war put a stop to his football. In France and Belgium he had little opportunity to play, but in the more serious business, he was awarded the Belgium Medal of Honour for bravery in action. Returning to Blackpool after the war he was elected captain, but in March 1920 he was surprisingly transfer listed, and Sheffield Wednesday splashed out a club record fee to take him to Hillsborough. In five seasons he accumulated 196 League and Cup appearances, and despite operating in a Second Division team that failed to rise above mid table, he was awarded 12 full England Caps, captaining his country on several occasions, and additionally representing the Football League in five matches. He was awarded a benefit of £650 at the close of the 1924-25 season, but following a dispute over terms for a new contract he departed Hillsborough and, to the amazement of the football world, joined Nelson for a fee that constituted a record for a Third Division club. He served the Seedhill club for five years prior to retirement, making 160 League appearances and scoring 18 goals. As was the case with many footballers of his generation, he worked as a licensee in both Nelson and finally in Blackpool, where he sadly died, very shortly after retiring in 1961.
Appearances: FL: 88 apps 13 gls FAC: 6 apps 0 gls Total: 94 apps 13 gls
Honours: England International, 12 caps 1921-24. Football League representative, five appearances.

WINSTANLEY, George
Inside right
Born: Blackpool, July quarter 1875
Died: 1898
Debut v Loughborough Town (a) 30.1.97, lost 1-4
CAREER: Blackpool October 1896. South Shore August 1897.

A serious mid term injury to Blackpool's inside right Sam Donnelly gave George Winstanley an initial opportunity in the eleven that visited Loughborough. His partner on the right wing, Nicholas Gillett, was making only his second senior appearance, and centre forward George Colville, normally a right half back, replaced Jack Parkinson at centre forward. Perhaps unsurprisingly the line failed to function as a unit, and the 'Luffs' ran out easy winners by a 4-1 score line. On the following Saturday, in a friendly match against Barnsley St Peter's at Raikes Hall, before a 'handful' of spectators, Winstanley scored Blackpool's fifth goal in the 5-1 win. His final senior outing, on 27th February, was at inside right in the 3-0 victory against Leicester Fosse.
Appearances: FL: 2 apps 0 gls Total: 2 apps 0 gls

WOLSTENHOLME, Arthur

Inside-forward
5' 8" 12st 0lbs
Born: Middleton, 14 May 1889
Died: Manchester, January quarter 1958
Debut v Leeds City (h) 1.1.10, won 3-1
CAREER: Tonge FC. Oldham Athletic

March 1908. **Blackpool December 1909**. Gillingham August 1912. Norwich City June 1913. Lincoln City July 1914. Wartime guest with Oldham Athletic 1915. Oldham Athletic May 1919, fee £75. Newport County June 1920. Darlington June 1921. Nelson May 1922, appointed to training staff season 1923-24, coach July 1925. Colne Town September 1926.

Arthur Wolstenholme began with Oldham Athletic while still in his teens, scoring ten goals in 26 League appearances in 1908-09. After losing his place in the following year he made the first of many subsequent moves to Blackpool. Rarely absent from the first team and adept in a variety of positions, his game featured shrewd passing and the ability to engineer openings for his colleagues. On leaving Blackpool he embarked on a wandering path, changing clubs annually on either side of World War One. He was the first player to score four goals in a Third Division North match when Darlington netted seven against Chesterfield on 10th September 1921. Nelson's player-manager David Wilson was a former playing colleague of Arthur Wolsenholme during his time with Oldham Athletic, and was well aware of his qualities. 13 goals in 36 matches was his excellent contribution to Nelson's Third Division North title winning side in 1922-23, and he remained at Seedhill in a coaching career when his lengthy playing career ended.
Appearances: FL: 77 apps 13 gls FAC: 5 apps 2 gls Total: 82 apps 15 gls
Honours: Nelson, Third Division North champions 1923.

WOLSTENHOLME, Thomas 'Tom'

Left half back
5' 10"   12st 0lbs
Born: Little Lever, 2nd February 1882
Died: 1956
Debut v Glossop (h) 11.10.02, drawn 2-2
CAREER: Farnworth Wednesday 1897. Everton amateur 1899. Blackpool Wednesday. **Blackpool September 1902**. Bolton Wanderers May 1905. Burnley June 1907. Bradford P.A. June 1908. Nelson August 1910.

Tom Wolstenholme first attraction the attention of the Blackpool committee towards the close of season 1901-02 when playing in a Medal Competition match, and before the season ended he had assisted the team in two friendly games. He signed a professional form just before the start of season 1902-03, and quickly showed his worth. Born at Little Lever, at the age of 15 he was playing regularly for Farnworth Wednesday – a team of shop assistants. Two years later he signed an amateur form with Everton, but as he secured a good business position in Blackpool, he only played twice for Everton Reserves. Blackpool Wednesday then had the benefit of his services before he was signed by Blackpool. Though only 19 years of age, he was a well-developed youth, who became a popular figure in Blackpool's middle line with his clean kicking and timely tackling. Following an 'ever present' season in 1904-05, a move to Bolton Wanderers brought only nine League appearances, but he found more opportunities with Burnley (38 appearances) and Bradford Park Avenue (39 appearances and one goal). Sam Wolstenholme, the Everton international was his brother.
Appearances: FL: 93 apps 0 gls FAC: 8 apps 0 gls Total: 101 apps 0 gls

WRIGHT. Jonathan William 'Bill'

Goalkeeper
5' 10½"   12st 0lbs
Born: Banks, Southport
Debut v Lincoln City (a) 22.11.02, won 2-0
CAREER: South Shore Swifts. Union Star. Lytham F.C. **Blackpool August 1902**. St Cuthbert's (Churchtown). Lytham Institute September 1904. Oldham Athletic May 1905. Southport Central cs 1908. Accrington Stanley September 1913. Manchester United September 1914.